Look For Rainbows

An Anthology of Queer Hope

QStory Northampton

ISBN: 979-8-3986-3251-4

Credits:

Editing:	Liz Simpson, Kit Nicholas
Proofreading:	Kit Nicholas, Jodie Neely
Cover Design:	Liz Simpson
Blurb:	Jodie Neely
Production Design:	QStory Northampton

Dedication

For all the LGBTQIA people around the world
who are in need of hope.

Introduction

When it rains look for rainbows seemed like a very appropriate saying for an anthology of queer stories on the theme of hope. Even now, too often the stories told about us are tragic and focused on struggles related to being LGBTQIA, but that wasn't what our local queer writing group wanted to produce. We agreed that, especially in these difficult times where many people are facing their basic rights being challenged, we need to read about queer people who lead hopeful (even happy!) lives, in spite of the difficulties they may face.

We formed our writing group, QScribe, under the umbrella of QStory Northampton in 2020 to support local people from our community who wanted to explore creative writing. The group is member-run and free to attend. We are really proud of how it has grown and established itself as a positive creative force in our lives. Our members are so encouraging and inventive that it is a joy to be a part of. We have different levels of experience – from those who've already been professionally published, to those picking up a pen again for the first time in many years – but all contribute to the success of the group.

When we decided to publish an anthology by

ourselves, there was a lot to consider. To start with, could we fit all our different styles and genres into one collection? We decided to give it a go and to choose a loose theme to draw our stories together. We wanted everyone to have the chance to show what they can do and conjure up whatever worlds they wanted to explore, without restricting their inventiveness. The result is an inspiring mix of queer characters and stories: from a spy thriller to coming-of-age stories to modern-day romances to horror and finally to a fantasy world where even dragons may live in hope.

We have enjoyed working on this project for the last year and are delighted to be able to share the results with you. It's been exciting to see how all our stories have developed over the course of our feedback sessions and how we can support each other to improve our craft. It's tested our skills and encouraged us to develop new ones as we've put together our first book without any outside help: everything you see has been created and honed by our members. We are really proud of our achievement and are launching it to coincide with our local Pride celebrations.

If you are looking for a supportive, inclusive writing group for LGBTQIA people or have ever thought about trying your hand at creative writing, you would be most welcome to join us. We host monthly meetups where we learn about different writing-related topics or share our works-in-progress. You could even feature in our next anthology! Find out more on our website, join our mailing list or follow us on our socials:

https://qstorynorthampton.wordpress.com/

northamptonqueerlitfest@gmail.com

Facebook   @qstoryn

Twitter   @qstoryn

Instagram   @qstoryn

Kit Nicholas,
QStory Northampton Chair

CONTENTS

A Little Bird Told Me

by Briony Hastings

Sunday

Ingrid put on her glasses and methodically adjusted her long woollen stockings, ensuring the tops of them were hidden beneath the hem of her demure grey skirt. She cast around for lipstick and eventually found it hidden beneath the battered newspaper on her dressing table. She applied it mechanically, no longer needing to check in the mirror. Six years ago, the make-up had felt like a fun disguise – all part of her new identity. Now her face looked odd without it.

The room behind her was dingy and cluttered. She hadn't bothered to open the curtains. A few discarded pieces of clothing hung limp and crumpled from her chair, while papers spilled over her desk and into an open drawer. Her typewriter was barely visible under the deluge.

Bruno gave an impatient whine outside her bedroom door.

She inched it open a crack. Bruno's eager

woolly face shone up at her, his tail beginning an enthusiastic wag. She raised an eyebrow. "Be patient," she told him, then closed the door again.

Phoenix had given her Bruno. Back when she'd first started this assignment. Back then, she'd said he'd be a useful cover. Now, the miniature black Schnauzer was the only friend she had within at least a hundred miles.

She perched a small grey hat on her carefully manufactured curls and grabbed her handbag.

Bruno sat up in excitement as she opened the door once more. His dark eyes gleamed in his greying fur.

"Come along then," she said.

The park wasn't far from her apartment. Even with her coat on, the morning felt chilly. The sky was dark and leaden. She went for their usual walk around the pond, smiling politely to passersby. As she passed the war memorial, she noticed a new stripe of scarlet graffiti. She averted her eyes. One of her heels crunched a thin layer of ice on a dirty puddle.

Eventually she took her seat on the cold, shabby bench and adjusted her stockings again. Bruno flopped down at her feet, panting.

"You're getting old," she told him, and

reached her hand surreptitiously beneath the bench. Her fingers brushed cold pockmarked steel and she pressed the hidden box in the right spots to release the lid. A quick swipe of her fingers and she shut it again.

It was empty. It had been empty for the last twenty-one months.

There had been periods of silence before. Six months at the longest. After that Phoenix had promised her that she would never have to wait so long again. But now, that promise was broken, crushed like the ice splinters beneath her shoe. And Ingrid was trapped. Far beyond enemy lines, in a cover so deep that sometimes she worried she'd never be able to emerge.

Bruno whined. Ingrid slid a small book from her handbag, pretended to read it for twenty minutes, and then began the walk back to her dishevelled apartment.

Thursday

The small shop bell rang jauntily as she pushed open the door of the café. Her glasses momentarily fogged up at the edges as they met with the rush of warm, sweet-smelling air. A couple sitting nearby glanced up and she smiled apologetically for the disturbance.

Ingrid took a seat at her usual table, ordered a coffee and a pastry, and settled down to read the paper. She had a little while before she was due to start work.

Back when she'd received coded messages, they had appeared in the obituaries section of the local paper. Not wanting to seem suspicious, or overly morbid, she'd sat and read through most of the paper to reach them. Now, though the messages were long gone, it had become a habit. Not to mention, she couldn't help but hope that one day the communication would resume.

She sat with the paper and studiously read through the front page. She sipped her hot strong coffee, set it down, and broke off a corner of the soft flaky pastry. She turned to the second page.

The headline *Foreign Spymaster Arrested* made her stomach drop through the floor.

Ingrid felt as though she was rushing backwards. Despite the warmth of the room, her hands felt suddenly very cold. She struggled to maintain her grip on the pastry. She was receding back into her own body, shrinking smaller and smaller, barely able to stare out from the deep recesses of her eyes.

She blinked, breathed, tried to steady herself.

4

Heard the noises of the café come into focus again: the clink of the cups in the kitchen behind her, the low murmur of conversation from the other patrons, the scrape of a fork against a plate.

Her first read-through of the article was so rapid as to be almost entirely useless, her eyes sliding off the words as if she were in a dream. The only thing that she managed to pick up was the name – *they had her real name.* Or at least, the name Ingrid had known her by in those rare dark, private moments.

She nibbled at the piece of pastry and tried again, forcing herself to slow down enough to glean the relevant information. She was a professional, after all. This time she managed to ascertain that:

1. Phoenix had been caught near the border.

2. She had been in custody for two months.

3. Or at least that was what the counterintelligence services had announced to the public.

4. The paper was celebrating this as the 'final blow' against an 'insidious network of subversives, traitors, and foreign operatives'.

"More coffee?" the waitress asked.

Ingrid jumped and her teacup rattled on its

saucer. She forced a smile. The waitress was pretty and fresh-faced. Very cheerful too, but Ingrid had only seen her working here for a few weeks. Her hair was trimmed close to her head in a fashionable cut and she was wearing a chequered apron. There was a barely detectable smear of flour on her right cheekbone and she was smiling a little apologetically.

"Sorry, no thank you. I should be getting to work soon."

"Not to worry." The waitress headed back towards the kitchen and Ingrid turned back to the paper.

There was nothing much of interest in the rest of it and, of course, nothing in the obituaries. She finished her cup of coffee and headed out into the dreary autumn air.

It was only a short walk to the Ministry of Foreign Affairs.

Ingrid showed her faded badge to the disinterested guard at the front desk and laboriously climbed the back stairs to the minister's office. As usual, the minister himself was absent. There was a stack of untidy, handwritten notes on her otherwise immaculate desk, a note that said 'Be here at five for dictation', and her trusty typewriter. Ingrid took off her hat, sat down, and got to work.

The typing was soothing, after a while. The trouble was that it was hypnotic enough to allow her mind to drift.

She remembered the day that Phoenix had found that this job was coming up. Her memory clumsily recreated the scene piece by piece, like an inexperienced artist attempting to sketch a beautiful vista.

"It's perfect!" Phoenix said, with an extravagant hand gesture and an animated grin. She was standing in front of an enormous, wall-mounted map of the city, pointing out the office building, the apartment, and the park. It was winter. The little light that filtered into the repurposed classrooms was cold and had a strange blue tinge. Overhead, a fluorescent bulb cast a harsh light on to the room beneath. But Ingrid scarcely noticed. It was always too compelling to watch Phoenix like this. She was dynamic, irresistible. A born leader. It was easy to see how she'd got her name. She was like a flame – bright, burning, consuming; drawing foolish moths into her orbit.

"No one thinks of the secretary," she had continued. "You can sit there like a piece of the furniture. They'll imagine you're just a sweet, helpful young lady." Another flash of that brilliant smile. Her hair was like fire, too. A striking auburn, it tumbled to the shoulders of her perfectly-tailored blue suit. It framed her pale, perfect face and her hazel eyes. "What do you say, Finch?"

As Ingrid sat, typing, one memory cascaded into another. This time, the artist's sketch was too hurried to pick out a coherent image.

That auburn hair again. But this time, there was no blue suit. Pale shoulders, soft skin. The light was different too – warm and golden. Or maybe the warmth was just from the hot breaths in her ear, the weight of Phoenix's body in her lap. Clutching desperately for closeness, the heat of skin against skin, auburn hair falling into her eyes…

Ingrid snapped out of her reverie. She squinted for a moment at the words she was faithfully transcribing. Something about them had rung an alarm bell, deep in the recesses of her mind. She read the note. Troop movements, protestors, border security. She carefully finished typing it up and then removed the note from the pile.

She fumbled in her bag for her glasses case.

It had a soft interior, ostensibly for protecting the glasses. In reality, the edge of it folded back, revealing a tiny compartment. Just enough space to accommodate a tightly-furled piece of paper.

She resumed her typing and tried to keep her mind away from dangerous memories.

Come midday, she picked up her bag and headed back downstairs. Past the silent security guard. Down the street. Unlocked the door of her apartment.

If anyone ever asked (they didn't), she came back home over her lunch break to let Bruno out of the house. But she had other duties too.

She unlocked the second drawer of her desk. Inside was her microfilm camera. She set the note on the light table, turned it on, and arranged the overhead camera. She clicked once to capture the image, adjusted the note, and then took the picture again. It was safer to duplicate work rather than risk an image not developing properly. She clicked open the side of the apparatus to check the film – still plenty of room on that roll. Every now and again, she had to process the films. Setting up the chemicals was always a bore and she had to then find a place to keep the images. She had painstakingly concealed one batch in a set of hollowed-out pencils and another in a small metal container fixed beneath the lining of a suitcase.

Her business done, she methodically returned the note to her glasses case. She greeted Bruno, apologetic for ignoring his excitedly wagging tail. She took him outside for a few minutes in the damp grey street and then set off to return to work.

As she walked briskly back to the office, she was suddenly startled by a voice.

"Excuse me! Excuse me!"

She turned to see the waitress from the café, trotting along the street towards her. Ingrid approached cautiously and the waitress gave a rueful smile. She still had flour on her cheek.

"Sorry to bother you, ma'am. After you came in this morning, a gentleman popped in and asked after you. A friend of yours? He left a note."

She extended her hand. There was a pale cream envelope, very slightly crumpled, but still sealed.

"Oh, thank you," Ingrid said, bemused.

"My pleasure. I'll be getting back," the waitress said, with an air of relief, and scuttled back towards the door of the café as quickly as she'd arrived.

***

The mystery of the envelope haunted her all afternoon. Ingrid tried to remain focused on her typing. Tried to convince herself that she should wait until she returned home. But her curiosity was just too strong. At least in the minister's office she knew she wouldn't be monitored. He was far too paranoid to have any surveillance equipment pointed in his own direction.

The paper of the envelope was thick, but not embossed or patterned in any way. She sniffed it quickly: it smelt of the café but nothing else distinctive. She slid her nail carefully under the seal and withdrew the note cautiously. She kept it at arm's reach as she unfolded it, but no sinister powder tumbled out.

The notepaper, too, was plain. Less weight than the envelope, with a very light creamy colouration to it.

The message, though, was certainly eye-catching.

WE KNOW, in typewritten capitals.

Then, **THEY ARE WATCHING YOU**.

STAY ALERT.

At the bottom, it was signed with a single scarlet stripe of red lipstick.

***

Walking home after work that evening felt like navigating a minefield.

Every instinct that Ingrid possessed told her to keep a close and vigilant watch on her surroundings, to note if she was being followed, to discover the faces and agendas of those who were watching her.

But if anything about her seemed out of place, if she looked overly cautious or watchful, then she ran the risk of alerting the people pursuing her that she'd been tipped off. And she knew from experience that that might cause them to expedite their plans. An unsuspecting mark could be monitored for weeks at a time – even in counter-intelligence agencies, bureaucracy and indecision could hold up the inevitable. But if the mark got spooked then they might flee or cause trouble, so it was better to send an urgent memo to cut through the red tape and bundle them off the streets before they had time to develop any ideas.

Still, she couldn't help but let her eyes linger on every passerby, on every silhouette in a doorway. If she were watching this street, she'd get some height – rent out one of the apartments above the local shops and settle in for a long stakeout. It was unusual for pedestrians to glance up to windows high above them, which made it an ideal hiding place.

Once she got home, she locked the apartment door behind her and immediately slid to the floor, curling her knees up to her chest. As she hid her face, she heard the patter of feet, a soft whine, and then felt a wet nose nuzzle concernedly under her arm.

"Bruno," she said. "What are we going to do?"

Friday

Her microfilm pencils had been collected together and stored in an unobtrusive metal case in her handbag. Likewise, she had ripped the storage container out of her suitcase and painstakingly sewn it into the lining of her handbag. She'd folded her identity documents and concealed them in a (genuine) half-full packet of cigarettes. If, somehow, she did manage to make it to a friendly contact, she needed some way to prove who she was. She felt the absence of a weapon particularly keenly.

But more importantly, she had come to some conclusions:

1. It was imperative that she continued with her life as normal to avoid additional suspicion.

2. If any enemy agents searched her apartment, it was going to be impossible to conceal who she was. It wasn't as if she had any innocent explanation for a foreign microfilm camera.

3. She had an escape route from the apartment – out of the back window, down the fire escape, using the curtain rope she'd stashed there. It wasn't ideal and any agent worth their salt would cut off all potential exits before knocking on her door. She just had to hope that they underestimated her.

4. If everything went wrong, then she had a tiny glass ampoule hidden in the left temple tip of her glasses. Meeting Bruno's worried eyes, she hoped she'd never have to use it.

She only worked four days a week, with the very occasional weekend thrown in, fitting around the other secretary in the minister's office, Anne. Their paths very rarely crossed and they communicated only in notes. Maybe Anne had children to look after, other commitments, or even another job. It was easy for Ingrid to be flexible and work around her. Her own commitments were significantly less demanding these days.

So she headed to the park, as was normal for her days off. For the majority of her walk, she worried about whether her departure time was entirely typical. It was only once she reached the park that she remembered the war memorial. The stripe of red paint was still adorning it, though this time a grey-uniformed worker was dully scrubbing at it, apparently without much success. Last time she'd assumed it was just a demonstration of random vandalism. Now, she wasn't so sure.

As she walked round the pond, she saw more red stripes, each now staffed by an unamused bucket-wielding attendant. One on the rim of a fountain, another daubed on the trunk of a tree. There were more passersby too, gathered around them – talking amongst themselves or even asking questions of the cleanup crew. A tall man in a hat seemed to be telling one particularly large group to leave.

Ingrid averted her eyes and continued walking.

She was relieved to see that her bench hadn't been vandalised. She sat down on the cold, slightly rain-spattered metal and reached underneath, her heart beating very fast.

The hidden box opened beneath her hand. Her fingers found a folded piece of paper and she winced as the sharp edge cut the tip of her index finger. But she drew it out, under the guise of adjusting her position on the bench, and slipped it between the pages of her book.

WE ARE WORKING TO EXTRACT YOU. STAY HIDDEN.

That stripe of lipstick again. What might it represent? She'd never seen a symbol like that used in her home country, or under Phoenix's department. Were they an external organisation? A different foreign power, even? Or were they a domestic rebel group, working against their own government? She had no idea.

She quickly turned the page of her book to hide the note, even as hope bloomed hot and aching in her chest. Could it really be possible? Terrifyingly, she could feel her eyes burning with tears, even as she attempted to seem engrossed in her book. Bruno stared plaintively up at her and it was all she could do to resist seizing him with both hands, lifting him into the air and crying to him that they were going home.

She drew in a long, cold breath, tried to focus on the words on the page, and willed herself to stay calm.

When might they be coming to get her – today, tomorrow, in a month's time? Was a member of the uniformed cleanup crew about to bundle her out of the way and lead her to safety? Or would she have to continue to wait indefinitely? How would she be able to tell friend from foe? What if this was all a setup somehow? What if they had managed to extract her identity from Phoenix? Or what if the government tracked her down before this elusive organisation (or individual) managed to save her?

Ingrid didn't have the answer to any of her questions. She sat and turned the pages of her book for twenty minutes, and then she headed back home.

***

There were no further developments for the rest of the day, though she remained on tenterhooks. She wasn't sure whether a knock on her door would mean salvation or that she would need to leap out of her back window with Bruno in her arms. She had a sense of building pressure, an atmosphere of anxiety and expectation. She couldn't settle to anything. Bruno stared at her, concerned and helpless, as she jumped at every noise and feverishly tidied the apartment for the first time in months. She wanted to go outside, but that wasn't entirely usual for her afternoon, so instead she peered out of her window, looking out desperately at the grimy street, as if expecting masked figures to leap from the rooftops and head with purpose towards her.

She spent the evening slumped exhaustedly at her desk, planning and re-planning potential escape routes out of the city and across the border, until she fell into a fitful sleep.

Saturday

There was no update, no contact, no knock on the door. The workmen at the park were still struggling with the red graffiti. The soldiers were out, apparently to prevent people from congregating and speculating. Ingrid kept her head down.

Sunday

There was a fresh stripe of red, this time across the park gates. There was a group of soldiers there too, apparently stopping people to ask them questions. A handful of young men there started arguing about it. The soldiers squared up, in formation, weapons already raised. Ingrid quickly diverted her route away from the park, despite Bruno's whine. She heard barked orders and the discontent of the growing crowd. She didn't look back.

She couldn't sleep for hours that night, restless and apprehensive. Bruno sensed her weakness and came to scratch on the bedroom door. Against her better judgement, she let him jump onto the bed and the comfort of his presence lulled her to sleep.

Monday

Naturally, her disturbed night caused her to oversleep on Monday morning. She didn't have time to visit the café before work and she never usually went on her lunch break.

The missed opportunity to collect a newspaper irritated her all day. She struggled not to slam down her typewriter keys in frustration.

She was also anxious without Bruno by her side. What if she had to leave work suddenly, without him? But bringing him in with her would be too suspicious. The thought of leaving him behind made her heart ache.

When she walked past the park that evening,

the gates were chained shut.

Tuesday

She was a little early to the café in the morning, but she couldn't bear to wait any longer. Brisk and self-possessed, she didn't linger to survey the pastries, but made a beeline for her usual table. The waitress bustled over with a smile. Ingrid ordered a coffee and snatched up the newspaper.

"Excuse me," she said politely, as the waitress returned holding the coffee pot. "This is yesterday's paper?"

"Oh, sorry about that," the waitress said blithely. "Let me go into the back and see if we have the new copies yet."

She left, and Ingrid was left in peace to skim the headlines. There was no mention of the graffiti in the park, or the soldiers on the streets, or any more activity from the counterintelligence services. Not that that was unusual. And there was no mention of Phoenix either. She'd had her day in the headlines and then been promptly forgotten. The paper featured only the normal local celebrities, schoolchild achievements, and the factories achieving their (mandatory) targets.

It didn't seem real, somehow, that life was just continuing on as normal. Ingrid felt off-balance, almost dizzy. She glanced towards the kitchen, but the waitress hadn't emerged yet. She turned, out of habit more than anything, to the obituaries.

STEPHEN BLACKWELL. Flew many stunning flights spanning numerous campaigns. Fought alongside Francis "Spike" Bachmann. Ejected, tortured, almost sunk. But never defeated. Never forgotten.

It sounded odd, but then the obituaries section did charge by the word.

Ingrid checked the second letter of each word, and then applied the seven-place left shift for the cypher.

MEET ME IN THE KITCHEN.

It was the cypher she and Phoenix had used.

Ingrid felt numb and spellbound. She left the paper and the half-eaten pastry at the table, and walked obediently to the side-door that led to the café's kitchen. Strangely, it seemed dark inside. She pushed open the door, walked inside and closed it behind her. All light was extinguished. The tiles echoed with her footsteps.

"Phoenix?" she breathed.

There was a moment of pause, then fluorescent lights flickered into life.

"No," the waitress said from the other side of the room, with a silenced pistol pointed in Ingrid's direction. "Just someone who knows the cypher."

"What...? How...?" Unarmed, Ingrid raised her hands in the air, her brain scrambling frantically to catch up.

"I need to check you're not a plant." The waitress was still wearing her chequered apron, but she held the gun with confidence and expertise. There was something calculating in her brown eyes. "There's not much time. Cook's only out on a smoke break."

"I cannot reveal..." Ingrid began.

"You will reveal," the waitress snapped, and she cocked the pistol. "And don't you make a move for your glasses either. I'll be honest with you, if you're honest with me. What is your codename?"

Ingrid stared at her. Her neatly arranged dark brown hair, her bright red lipstick. "The note was from you?"

The waitress inclined her head. "Yes, I lied about acting as a messenger for some gentleman friend, if that's what you mean. What is your codename?"

Ingrid allowed that small, warm spark of hope to flare in her chest.

"My codename is Finch," she said. "Don't shoot."

"And what was the name of Phoenix's second-in-command?"

All the tensed muscles in Ingrid's body relaxed at the recognition of the code-phrase.

"The fire has no master and no lieutenant."

The waitress lowered the gun immediately and put the safety on. "Thank fuck. Right, we have to go."

"You're here to extract me?"

"Yes. I've been working here three weeks seeing if we were confident enough in your identity to make contact. We were all ready to go yesterday, but you never turned up. I thought they'd already got you. We can't wait any longer."

"What's the plan?"

"There's a car parked two streets over." The waitress ripped off her apron, stuffed it into a bag, and pulled out a dark shawl to drape around her head. "We go there now, before you're late for work. Then we drive straight for the border and we hope our contact is still there to sneak us through."

"I can't go now," Ingrid blurted.

"You *what*? You want to say goodbye to your boss, or shake hands with the soldiers at West Park, or — "

"My dog," Ingrid said. "My dog is still in my apartment. I can't leave him..."

The waitress looked distinctly unimpressed. "I thought you were a professional. Fine. I'm not waiting here. You go and get him, and meet me at forty-three Vincent. I'll get your bag from the café. If you're not there in ten minutes, we're leaving without you."

"What's your name?" Ingrid asked desperately.

"Call me Skylark. Now *go*."

Ingrid ran without caution or restraint. Passersby raised their heads belatedly as she passed. The air was cold in her lungs and the pavement was hard beneath her feet, and *she was going home*.

She reached the edge of the street and hesitated for a fraction of a second. Left was the shorter route, but it took her past West Park. She turned right instead. She dodged past a group of briefcase-carrying businessmen, past the stream of gloomy commuters, even two or three of the uniformed cleaners.

She reached the front door of the apartment building, still at a full sprint. The world swayed for a moment as she stopped dead and fumbled for her keys in her pocket. She fought to keep the key steady in the lock, pushed open the door, and then ran up the stairs towards the apartment. As she reached her door, she could hear Bruno's whining and scratching, as if he knew the urgency of the situation.

"Bruno, Bruno," she muttered, as she wrenched open the door and he jumped into her arms, both of them shaking with anxiety and anticipation. "Come on, come on, we need to go."

She didn't bother locking the apartment door. She stumbled down the steep stairs, flung open the front door, and began running again. Bruno seemed to forget his years and joined her in the sprint.

Left from the front door, left again toward their destination. Her side ached with a stitch, her breaths came in ragged gasps, tasting of blood. She glanced back again to check on Bruno and stumbled awkwardly, causing a pang in her ankle. But she couldn't let it stop her.

She veered right, cutting across the road in

front of a queue of pedestrians. Someone yelled: "You! Stop!" She ignored them. She could feel her heartbeat in the palms of her hands, in her flushed cheeks. Every jolting step sent pain through her ankle, but she couldn't stop.

The dark grey car was pulled over on the right-hand-side. She slowed for a second to let Bruno scramble up into her arms and then she heard the car's engine start. For a second she felt the cold fingers of doubt grasp at her chest, but then she saw a flame-red head in the backseat turn towards her.

The rear left door was flung open and she jumped inside without missing a beat, swinging it shut behind her. She and Bruno spilled into the back seat, sliding on old, musty leather. Bruno immediately flopped into the footwell, panting. But Ingrid only had eyes for the person in the seat beside her.

"Phoenix, how...?"

Phoenix smiled. She looked older. A little tired. There was a scar running along her temple that she hadn't had before. Ingrid went to touch it, before she restrained herself.

"It's a long story. But there'll be plenty of time to tell it on the way home."

Ingrid lunged forwards for an embrace. The car's indicator clicked to begin its journey out of the city. And Ingrid let her racing heart calm as she held Phoenix in her arms.

Author Bio

Briony (she/her) is a bisexual woman in her twenties. She began writing at the age of six when she dutifully composed a long rip-off of the Famous Five, and she hasn't stopped since. She reads and writes a range of genres (especially historical and mystery fiction), but particularly loves delving into fantasy worlds.

When she's not writing poetry as the resident bard of her Dungeons and Dragons party, she enjoys swimming, baking, and tending to an untidy vegetable garden that began as a research project for a long-abandoned novel.

Beyond the Music
by Kit Meredith

The vibrations flowed through Cass, emanating from the cello they were curled around and the music surrounding them. They let themself be drawn in completely so the lines between their body and the wooden instrument blurred. The music seemed to come directly from them, an extension of them, and their consciousness was swept up in it. And they weren't alone: they were connected to the other players in the ocean of sound they'd all created, swaying together in its current. Cass leaned towards the viola player to their right, locking eyes for a moment as their song connected them through the vibrating air. They held onto the connection, leaning into it, revelling in being more than they were alone.

When the piece ended, they held their position with their bow in the air, not wanting to stopper the last note as it rang clear. Not wanting to hasten the moment when their connection to the others would fade with it. They closed their eyes and savoured the last ring, until they couldn't tell if it was still going or just an echo inside their mind. Which meant it was time to open their eyes to the world again. Cass reluctantly let them creep open and slumped back in their seat, ready for the onslaught of chatter and tuneless movement.

Except when they opened them, the viola player was still there too. And she was gazing at them in a way that kept a spark of the connection going.

Who was she? Cass scoured their memory for her face but couldn't find it. She must be new: everyone else was at least familiar even if Cass didn't remember many of their names (and it was far too late to ask). The community orchestra didn't get a big turnover of players, though sometimes newbies would flit in and out. For the main part it was comfortably stable and no-one paid Cass too much attention. They had their place as a stalwart of the cello section; good but not brilliant. Good enough, which was all they wanted to be. But the newbie was looking at them as if she saw something more interesting. Then she smiled, stood up and stepped closer.

"Hi!" She kept looking at Cass, while loosening the hairs of her bow with a twist of the end.

"Hi," Cass echoed, twisting their own bow until they looked down and saw the hairs were so wilted they seemed in danger of dropping off.

"I don't think we've been introduced. I'm Devon, she/her. I just moved back to the area." Her smile faltered, but so slightly that if Cass hadn't been studying her lips, they may have missed it. "For now, anyway."

Devon followed this up with a shrug that was open to interpretation. Was it meant to invite questions or keep them away: the start of a story or the wish to avoid telling one? Cass couldn't be sure so it was best play it safe.

"I'm Cass, they/them. Good to have you join us." They needed to put down the bow before the sweat building in their palms infiltrated it. They attempted to place it discretely on the music stand but it clattered as they misjudged the distance, distracted by Devon's vibrant presence.

With her short, stylishly scruffy hair and tattooed ink creeping out from under her loose tee, she wasn't the orchestra's usual kind of recruit. Classical musicians tended to look more ... classical. Not hot, queer-looking women that sent sparks flying even without the use of an instrument. Cass tried to shrug off the line of thought. *You should not be perving on the newbie.* Devon was probably just being friendly and had picked out the other young-looking, queer-looking member of the group. The pronouns in her intro hinted so.

"Are you coming along for drinks after we pack up? Someone said you usually head to a nearby pub."

Some of the members did, but Cass didn't usually go anywhere other than home after rehearsals. They had gone along a few times, but without the music embracing them and tethering them to the group, they inevitably felt like an outsider when immersed in the others' heteronormative, neurotypical world views. It was hard to feign interest for long in all the things they didn't want – marriage, babies, exotic holidays ...

Maybe that was why Devon asked them? Maybe she would feel as lost as they did and wanted someone there that she had a better chance of connecting with.

Maybe if they went along, they could help ensure Devon wanted to come back.

"Sure," they said, affecting a casual tone that shouldn't let on that this wasn't their usual response. *If it's really uncomfortable, you can leave after one drink. You can manage one drink.*

"Great!" Devon's smile blazed like she meant it.

A warm, fuzzy feeling settled in Cass's stomach amidst flutters of panic. They had just agreed to go for a drink with the most intriguing new addition to their (semi-) social circle in a long time. And they had no time to prepare: to change into something more flattering or rehearse a script. Great.

***

Cass regretted it as soon as they stepped inside the pub. It was stuffy and loud, despite only being half full. There was a prominent jukebox connected to a central sound system pumping background music around the whole venue. They tried to spy out a corner that was free from speakers and might give them a chance of being able to engage in conversation.

Meanwhile their fellow musicians had already started to get drinks and had claimed a few tables down one side of the long room, so that was that. At least they had some ear plugs stashed in a jacket pocket that could take the edge off. Though they didn't fancy trying to explain how they loved to get absorbed into the centre of the chamber orchestra's sound but couldn't cope with loud music otherwise. Or at least distracting music which they were expected to filter out while trying to decipher the intricate meanings of what was being said. They could nip into the toilets to put them in discretely. The gendered public toilets. They groaned. Why hadn't they done it while they were still in the relative safety of the community centre?!

"It's not exactly to my taste either, but I wouldn't say it's that bad." Devon had come up beside Cass without them realising that anyone was paying attention and must have caught their exhalation.

They jumped at the whisper in their ear and let out a nervous laugh, hoping it counted as an acceptable response.

"You could go line up some better tracks while I get the drinks, if you like."

Aha, so it was the cheesy, outdated pop music she thought they were objecting to. They could go along with that, except changing the tune wouldn't make the setup more bearable.

The door opened behind them, letting in a gentle coolness they wanted to glug down. They scanned the pub again and spotted a 'beer garden this way' sign. It was a mild summer evening, so that could work.

"Or we could sit outside. Fresh air would be nice."

"Good idea. I'll get the first round."

'First round' insinuated there'd be more than one. They should've pointed out they probably wouldn't stay to pay for the next one, but when they caught sight of the sparks still glinting in Devon's eyes, they closed their mouth again. Owing them a drink might not be a bad thing.

To get out to the beer garden they had to walk past where the others were sitting ... which meant they were at risk of peer pressure to join them. Cass waited for Devon to get the drinks, then let her go ahead. She didn't hesitate in moving past the huddle, with little smiles and nods of recognition. But not the beam of a smile she'd given Cass, or any invitation for the others to join them. Cass's pulse quickened.

Mercifully, the music didn't extend far into the courtyard, with only one speaker on low volume attached to the main wall.

"Where do you want to sit?" Devon paused to wait for directions.

"Over there looks good." Cass pointed to the farthest table, which rested against the wall and was set apart from the occupied ones.

Devon obediently strolled over to where they'd pointed, her viola case bumping against her butt, keeping rhythm with her steps. It took Cass longer than it should have done to realise they were staring. They hadn't been admiring her butt, but now they were thinking about it ... *Nope, eyes up.*

Once she'd set her drink down, Devon half-removed her viola and stared at the wooden bench, as if scoping out whether it was a safe resting place for the precious instrument.

"Did you not want to leave that in your car?" Unless she didn't have car. Should they offer to put it in theirs for safe keeping or would that be too forward?

"No. Not that I don't trust people round here, but it's worth far too much to risk it." Her voice dropped to a low murmur, contradicting her declaration of trust.

"How much?" The question was out before they could consider if it was appropriate to ask. String instruments generally cost a lot – due to being hand-made rather than factory-made for anything above a beginner's instrument – but something about the way Devon said it made it seem less ordinary.

"Now that would be telling."

Yes, it would. That's the point. They swallowed any outward objection to the redundant phrase.

"Let's just say, if I don't decide to go on with my professional career, selling it would put me in a good place to start over. If I could bear to part with it."

"You're a pro?!" What was a pro doing in their community group?

"Maybe … I was and I may go back, but I'm taking a break. I wasn't sure it was right for me anymore. I was losing the love of it."

"How long are you taking off?"

"Right now, I genuinely have no idea. I'm holding off deciding for as long as I can, though as that involves crashing back at my parents' place I may not end up taking too much time."

"Fair enough." Cass couldn't imagine moving back into their busy family home, having adjusted to living alone in blissful peace.

They took a sip of their coke, bubbles fizzing against their top lip, then placed the clammy glass back down well away from the edge of the table. They didn't want to risk embarrassing themself by knocking it over with their loose limbs and it seemed doubtful that Devon would forgive them if it contaminated her precious cargo.

"That's not what I want to think about right now though. Tell me about you."

The quick change in conversation made Cass blink and they had to take a moment to adjust. *What did she want to know?*

Devon seemed to note their hesitation and offered a prompt. "What are you doing in this corner of the world? I don't remember you from growing up here and I'm pretty sure I would."

She said it with a suggestive lilt that brought heat to Cass's cheeks, even though they suspected it wasn't true. They'd done their best not to stand out at school, and if Devon had noticed them it likely wouldn't have been a fond memory given the awkward teenager they'd been, with their clumsy body and clumsy words. Not that they were much different now, but they'd grown into both and learned to accept them as part of their humanity. Even if the world still didn't. Getting their autism diagnosis had helped, plus moving on from the playground cliques and narrow expectations. But Devon was right, they'd thankfully not bumped into each other back then.

"I moved here for a teaching job, four years ago."

Maybe Devon had been flirting, but maybe not. Best answer the question literally, which was what came naturally. Cass could see how the evening went and whether there were any further hints of interest.

Not that the possibility was why they'd agreed to come. Or why they didn't hesitate when it came time to buy another round. Or why they stayed talking as the sky faded around them until it felt like the two of them were in their own cosy cocoon, glowing in the lamplight.

***

By the time the next rehearsal came around a week later, Cass had spent many hours revisiting their conversation with Devon and fantasising about getting to know her more. They were partially excited about the chance to see her again and partially worried that their excitement would be too obvious. They had always been told they wore their heart on their sleeve, which put it at risk of being easily bruised. They'd also never had the desire to engage in the mind games people unnecessarily brought into play when it came to dating. It overcomplicated things when they could be complicated enough already. Especially when you didn't know what you wanted from someone, only that they drew you in and you didn't want to resist the pull.

"Cass!" Devon called from the other side of the car park.

Was it bad that they'd known who it was before they'd turned to look, considering they'd only spent one evening with her? Cass tried to school their face to hide how much their stomach had flipped. *Play it cool, you've only just met.*

"Hey." They stopped to allow her to catch up, standing their cello case up and lightly hugging it for support.

"Hey." Devon beamed at them as she drew level. "How was your week?"

"Alright." Cass tried to think of something interesting to say but drew a blank, the last seven days fading from their mind in the glow of Devon's smile. "You?"

"Not bad. Been looking forward to heading back here. I know it's just a little community group, but it's still good to be playing with others again."

Cass felt their smile grow brittle and in danger of cracking. It may be just a 'little group' to Devon, but it was the bright point of their week. "Yeah, I suppose it must seem that way to you."

The air between them turned awkward so Cass turned away, heaving their cello back up over their shoulder and letting the firm weight settle.

"I didn't mean it like that. It's a great group! It's just different than what I'm used to."

Stop digging. The restatement still had a patronising air to it that Cass didn't want to let sink in. "We better get inside and set up." They didn't look at her again before heading in.

This time, Devon didn't attempt to catch up with them. It wasn't until she took her seat next to Cass that they acknowledged each other again with half smiles. Until the music started.

It took more than a few bars for Cass to slip under its influence, Devon's remarks having left it tainted. But they couldn't resist the lure for long and they sunk deep into the bath of vibrations, letting it lull them, letting it draw out the frustrations of another long week and another dismissive person, letting it all flood out and disperse in the sea of sound until there was nothing left but the music and they were the music, the pulse and flow of it as vital as the blood in their veins.

And there was Devon beside them, leaning in, reaching out to them with an irresistible mellow note, falling into rhythm and complementing them sensitively so they twined together without either overpowering the other, locked in a familiar dance. Cass found themself turning away from the conductor towards the expressive musician beside them who it seemed they could trust to keep them tethered to time. And when the last notes rang out, once again they held on to the connection, not wanting to even breathe and break the spell.

But they couldn't stay like that forever and the movement around them became too relentless to be ignored.

"I love Elgar, don't you?" Devon broke their silence.

The romantic composers, including Elgar, were Cass's favourite as they invited the outpouring of emotions that earlier styles restrained. But they couldn't find the words in that moment to explain … and were reticent to bring up the topic of romance.

"Yes. To play, anyway. It's not the same just listening." They'd managed to say something at least.

"I get you. It's not the same when you're not part of it. It doesn't grip me in the same way and I find my fingers twitching to join in."

"Exactly." Cass let out a long breath in relief. There was no judgement this time: maybe Devon wasn't a total snob who thought everyone should spend their time listening to Bach. Besides, she clearly didn't think they were rank amateurs if she was prepared to come back and slum it with them.

"So, are we heading to the same place as last time? Seems like another nice night to sit out under the stars."

Cass tried not to read too much into Devon's leading note and smile. But they didn't hesitate to say yes.

***

It was still hot outside when Cass found the poster advertising auditions for the Christmas concert. Which was odd, not because of the timing as it was normal to start rehearsing for their biggest concert of the year at the end of summer, but because they didn't usually do auditions except to screen new players.

"At least they've given us a couple of weeks to prepare." Devon bumped shoulders with them as she joined them staring at the A4 announcement. "Have you seen the sheet music yet?"

"No."

Cass shook off their confusion at the change in process. The reason for it was likely standing right next to them: no newbie would usually be given a lead part, but newbies weren't usually in Devon's league. None of them were.

The conductor must have been delighted at the chance to have a pro out front. And from the sounds of it, Devon wouldn't be letting him down. Lynn, the longstanding lead viola player, was unlikely to hang onto her well-earned spot. Or get the chance to play the grand viola part that must be on offer if the plan was to have Devon star. As much as Cass didn't want to put Devon off, the thought of Lynn being ousted was a barrier to any excitement they may have absorbed from her.

"You're going to audition, right?"

"Probably not." Cass shrugged and stepped back.

"Why not? You're ace, you'd totally be in with a shot."

"Auditions aren't my idea of fun. And I'm good, but I'm not that good. We aren't all prodigies." Despite being positive on the surface, it was one of the autism stereotypes they hated: it seemed people either saw you as useless or phenomenal, there was no human in-between. It was tempting to explain, but they didn't want to head into a rant.

"I disagree, I've heard you play, remember? I've seen how the music takes you. You're special."

There was no masking their response this time – Cass flinched at the word, despite Devon clearly meaning it as a compliment. They'd been called 'special' often enough to realise it most often wasn't one. At least they had turned away so Devon wouldn't have seen the shadow cross their face. She was trying to be nice and was the first new friend they'd made in a while. Especially the first new friend who made their stomach flutter in the good way. They closed their eyes and breathed slowly before twisting back round to reply.

"Thanks, but I'm not interested. If I was the lead, I couldn't lose myself in that way. And I don't need the attention." Too late, they realised that last part might have sounded like a dig.

"I guess that's where we differ. I've always been in the spotlight. To be honest, I feel a bit lost without it." Devon chuckled, but it had a sad ring to it.

"That makes sense. It must be a big adjustment for you."

Devon cocked her head to one side. "It doesn't sound like you're entirely convinced. Or is it just hard for you to imagine wanting that."

"No, it's not that, just ..." They knew they maybe shouldn't say it, even before the truth leaked out, "Lynn is great and it would be sad for her to lose her spot." Surely Devon could understand their torn loyalties: the orchestra, and everyone in it, had been a core part of their life long before she arrived.

"No-one's taking it off her and handing it to me. She gets to audition too, fair and square."

Okay, so maybe she couldn't understand. Maybe she'd never had anyone endanger her place and had always been the one doing the taking.

A few other members sidled up to look at the poster and interrupted their conversation, which was probably for the best. Cass didn't want to argue with Devon. This opportunity clearly meant something to her and it wouldn't be fair to ask her to let it go just because she would be usurping Lynn.

It was hard to pretend they were happy about the idea though. For the first time in a month, they didn't join the social after rehearsal and headed home before anyone could ask why.

***

By the next week, Cass was less set in their conviction and ready to face Devon again. They'd even started to wonder if they should give the auditions a try. It wasn't like they had anything to lose ... unlike Lynn. They tried not to think about Lynn: she could fight her own battles and didn't need them adding to any tension.

They were one of the first to arrive and were securely seated before the room started to fill. Matt, the lead cellist, arrived at the same time as Lynn and they turned their attention to him instead. He was a good leader: well-prepared, consistent and encouraging. Could they challenge him? The Christmas concert was the most well-attended of the year, but it wasn't everything. If they auditioned for the chamber quartet part in this, it didn't have to mean toppling him from the general leadership position.

The thought of playing the cello solo, even as part of a quartet involving Devon, sent a shiver down their spine. They tried to analyse it; whether it was the good or bad kind, excitement or dread, or both. But then Devon arrived and another trickle of sensations added to the confusion.

Matt seemed to notice them analysing him. "You know, if you decide to audition, I promise not to hold it against you. It's good for an old man to be challenged sometimes."

Cass laughed, grateful for the interruption to their introspection. At forty he was barely older than they were, though people struggled to age Cass in their androgyny.

"Does this mean you're reconsidering?" Devon had leaned over so far, her breath tickled their cheek.

"I don't know." Cass twisted to let her catch their eye. "I don't want to lose the joy by putting pressure on my performance."

It had accidentally sounded like an innuendo. Maybe it was one, in a way: they had been worrying whether trying to grow their budding connection could cause it to wither. They should just enjoy it, especially with the uncertainty over whether Devon would stay for long or disappear back to her high-pressure career that would leave little room for any sweetheart left behind.

The look on Devon's face was difficult to interpret but if they were to hazard a guess, they'd say she was overthinking something too. The conductor rapped his baton on his stand before they could analyse it any further and they soon lost their train of thought as they let themself sink into the music.

When the rehearsal ended, it was Devon who slipped away without explanation. She was probably heading off to practise. Maybe they could get back to how they'd been once the auditions were out the way. Maybe it wouldn't change anything between the two of them, even if she would be one seat further away.

***

The next week passed quickly as Cass's students returned from the summer holidays, not leaving much time for overthinking or preparing for the audition. By the time the big day came around, Cass hadn't had a chance to pick up their cello and was certain it was a good thing they hadn't been convinced to join in with the auditions. Music was their escape from the pressures of the world, not a place to add more.

When they took their seat for the usual group rehearsal, they felt calmer than they had since first setting eyes on the unsettling poster. They had their place where they belonged and there was absolutely no need to strive to change that.

Devon seemed calmer too. She didn't mention anything about the auditions and slipped straight into a standard weekly catch up.

When the baton rapped she whispered something about catching up properly later. Did that mean she was expecting Cass to stay on? They wanted to ask, but a downside of their front row seat was that they couldn't chat without the conductor getting annoyed. They'd never seen it as a downside before, preferring to stay out of the small talk and in the music, but maybe it was because they'd never had anyone they really wanted to talk to.

Despite the calmness Devon exuded when she sat down, once they started to play she was the opposite. It seemed like there was more emotion to her bow, every note a song in itself, and Cass realised that she must have been holding back before so as not to overshadow everyone else. They couldn't resist leaning in, letting themself be swept up in her song and the chord that thrummed between them. Cass wasn't special, but there was something more than ordinary in the way the music flowed when they joined with Devon. This was what they came for, to be swept up and be part of something greater than themself.

There was a curve to Devon's lips whenever they glanced at her; not her usual wide smile but one that seemed for herself only. Sometimes her eyes were closed and she seemed so bound to her song that Cass almost felt jealous. They lost count of the rest bars in their part as they gazed at her. Once, Matt even gave them a nudge with his foot to get them back on track. But it didn't work for long.

A break was called at the end of a particularly tricky movement, and while the others stood up to stretch and grab refreshments Devon stayed seated, leaning back with that private smile still on her face. When she finally opened her eyes, she turned straight to Cass and caught them staring.

"Hey," she said softly.

"Hey. You okay?"

She didn't seem upset exactly, but there was something different in her energy that Cass craved to understand.

"Yeah. Yeah, you know I think I really am." Her smile grew to include Cass.

"Good." They didn't know what else to say – they didn't want to come off too weird by commenting on her energy.

"I've been thinking about what you said last week, about not wanting to lose the joy. How that was the issue which had made me step back. Before I started to think about auditions, I was starting to get it back … which I have you to thank for."

"Me?" Cass blushed, happy to have brought Devon joy but not getting exactly how and if they could really take the credit.

"Yes, you." She poked them gently with her precious bow, which was probably worth more than their entire instrument. "The way you lose yourself in it and don't compete, just join with us in a way that makes the music feel palpable. And your refreshing honesty and openness in sharing that with me. I'd forgotten what that was like, to play for the love of it. So, thank you."

"You're welcome." Cass reached over and squeezed Devon's hand. Then froze, wondering if that was too forward.

But Devon turned her hand over and squeezed theirs back. And kept holding it.

"Fancy going out to celebrate after we finish here? Somewhere different? I didn't manage to have dinner beforehand and we could get something to eat. Unless you've already eaten?" Her speech was rushed, as if she was pushing out the invitation before she lost her nerve.

"No."

Devon's smile drooped and her hand lost its grip on theirs.

"No, I haven't eaten!" Cass scrambled to correct her apparent misunderstanding. "Yes, I would love to go for dinner with you."

"Awesome, it's a date!" She ran a thumb over Cass's palm and a shiver ran through it. Definitely the good kind.

"Awesome," they echoed. "Wait, what about the auditions, won't it be too late by the time you're done?"

"I'm not auditioning. I'm giving myself permission to enjoy myself instead. Finding the joy, remember? Unless you are, then I can wait for you?"

"No, I'm not either. I vote for enjoying ourselves."

It was a decision they'd already made, but even if they hadn't ... maybe a date with Devon would be worth changing their plans for. They might have been the one to remind Devon of the joy music could bring, but Devon had been the one to remind them of the joy of connecting with someone outside of it. Even if she didn't stick around forever, that seemed worth the risk.

And maybe, just maybe, their connection would last far beyond the rehearsal hall.

Author Bio

Kit Meredith (they/them) is an extroverted introvert who enjoys connecting with people through the arts. Neurodivergent and really very queer, they relish writing about characters who also live and love queerly.

Kit also enjoys crafting and making possibly too many things for other people. They are often found plugged into their headphones listening to a comedy-educational podcast or an audiobook, or just pretending to in order to avoid awkward small talk. They were delighted to find listening while doing chores allows them to fit more books into their life. They spend their life in service to their pampered pets.

See You Again
by Angela Nolan

On the day my life changed forever, I pulled up to an average looking house, my handbrake squealing in protest at being forced to work in such cold temperatures. My car was slowly falling apart, but my line of work didn't exactly pay well so I had to take what I could get. I slammed the car door, and the cold immediately bit at my face. I rang the bell, then realised I'd left my phone in the car but decided it was too cold to go back for it. That's something I've regretted almost every day since.

The door was opened by an elderly woman with kind eyes. She barely let me introduce myself before inviting me into the warmth. Far too trusting really, exactly the type of person I started offering my services for. As expected, her eyes changed from kind to clouded by suspicion as I mentioned that I knew she'd recently had an appointment with local "psychic" Lucky Luna. It was always hard to resist doing the air quotes when talking with one of her victims. A petite woman with long, blonde, frizzy hair and bright clothes in need of an iron turning up at your door wasn't an immediate threat, but when I revealed personal information people became wary. Before she could get too angry and ask how I knew, I revealed my true intentions and stopped her in her tracks.

"Rob sent me. He wants you to look inside Alice in Wonderland. He said he left a few messages, but you haven't found that one yet."

She stared at me, mouth slightly agape, before rushing off to the bookcase next to the dining table. As she flicked through the pages, an envelope dropped lightly onto the carpet. She ripped it open and read the letter inside, lips mouthing along as a small smile tugged at them and her eyes brimmed with tears. After she'd finished reading, she sank into a chair dabbing at her eyes with a tissue. She offered me a tea but her hands were shaking so I made it, being liberal with the sugar to help with her shock.

"Have you really spoken to him? He's been gone for almost four months, but I still feel him around," she croaked out.

"He speaks about you all the time. You can feel the love you have for each other." I squeezed her hand comfortingly and hoped my long-term partner, Erica, and I would be just as in love when we were elderly.

"How long have you been speaking to spirits?" she asked.

I launched into an explanation I'd given so many times it felt like giving my own name. "I've had this gift since I was a child. I tried to ignore it for a long time, but I realised as I grew up that there's a lot of people who pretend they're gifted to make a quick buck out of grieving people. That didn't sit well with me and I realised those trying to speak to me, as well as the living they left behind, deserved proper closure and I could provide it. So I learnt some basic hacking skills and broke into the client lists of the scammers in the area. They tend to crowd me a bit and their voices overlap which can get overwhelming, but if I provide the details of a loved one, that spirit comes into focus – sort of like tuning a radio. I can't offer a message to everyone but assuming their loved one is still around then I follow the path of the charlatans and deliver real goodbyes. I'd like to do more but there's only one of me."

I always begin to gabble a bit at this point as it's a lot of information to throw at a perfect stranger. Luckily, I'd grabbed some water when I made her tea so I chugged that down while the cogs whirred in her head processing what I'd told her. Her eyes were looking a bit misty again, but she wore a soft smile. I had no connection to her and there really was no way for me to know about the note so she should be convinced I was legit. Whether that was enough for her to abandon faith in the psychic she'd trusted before wasn't really my concern. I just try and restore hope for grieving people; I'm not after repeat business.

I've known about my gift since I was eight. I'd seen people who'd passed before that, but most of my schoolmates had imaginary friends so I assumed they fell into that category. Once my peers' friends began to fade away, however, mine only became stronger. The first time I realised what I could do with my abilities was when I told my teacher where to find her mother's locket that she'd been missing. I didn't really comprehend what I was saying, I just knew an elderly woman had been very persistent for the last few days. She was angry at first and kept grilling me on how I could possibly know. The following day though she turned up wearing a new necklace. She gently squeezed my hand and mouthed 'thank you' and I haven't looked back since.

After hearing about this woman's love affair with Rob and their life together for a little while, I walked back out to my car laden down with a crisp twenty, several books and a few jars of homemade jam. I can never bring myself to actually charge for my services, especially after these people have already shelled out in good faith for a fabricated message, but I always come away with something. Twenty pounds wouldn't buy me a new car any time soon but at least I could buy food this week.

Luckily I found a blanket in the boot to protect the jam and then as the engine sputtered to life and I cranked up the heating, I checked my phone. Four missed calls from my partner Erica, which kicked off my alarm bells as she knew I was with a client this morning. I had two voicemails, which I know she hates leaving so that made my stomach twist in knots further. I played the first, heard the name of a hospital and screeched off without waiting to hear the rest.

By the time I reached the hospital my heart was beating so fast I could hear blood roaring in my ears, and I screamed at the receptionist over the noise. I gave her Erica's name and then I was quickly led into a small quiet room, not the ward I expected. The doctor came in shortly after me and delivered terrible news in a calm soothing voice, which was a juxtaposition that's come up in my nightmares many times since. Erica had been in a car accident and was pronounced dead on arrival at the hospital. Realistically if I'd picked up the call earlier, I still wouldn't have been able to say goodbye but grief and guilt are a vicious combination that will have you second-guessing all your decisions.

I stayed in that room and sobbed until the quiet began to feel oppressive and I could no longer put off going back to our empty flat. I'm not ashamed to say I didn't leave the bed for a week, and then put off washing the sheets for far too long as I didn't want to remove her scent from our space. I missed everything about her. I missed her endless patience when my anxiety was lying to me and telling me everyone was against me. I missed the way her nose crinkled and her eyes shone when she laughed. I missed the way she always knew how to rescue my culinary failures.

Once I'd picked myself back up a little, I got a normal job frying burgers. It was boring and I came home stinking of grease, but my co-workers were fun and it paid the bills. I feel awful about it now, but I ignored those from the afterlife who came to me until they became frustrated enough and left. I just couldn't bear using my gift because there was only one person I wanted to see and she never appeared no matter how much I called out to her. Not until that fateful night anyway.

Erica had been gone two months when I first started noticing my belongings moving around. It was subtle, so it may have started earlier and I didn't register it, but every time I came home one or two things were out of place. I'm not the tidiest person but I like certain things to have set places to facilitate an easy routine. It's kind of funny how the smallest things can tip you over the edge when you're barely holding on to your sanity. I remember one day I sobbed on the bathroom floor because my face wash wasn't on the back of the sink, so my hand grabbed only air when I went to pick it up. I found it later inside the medicine cabinet, which isn't a place I've ever kept it. For a little while, I blamed myself and assumed I was still adjusting to having the space to myself and creating new routines.

As the weeks went on though, I began to be consumed by a white-hot rage. It had never happened before, they'd always just spoken to me, but I began to think it must be the spirits trying to get my attention because I'd been ignoring them. Whenever I noticed something in the wrong place, I would scream obscenities, threats and curses even if I couldn't see any ghosts in the vicinity. It's a good job my neighbours knew what I was going through as I dread to think how many noise complaints I would have received otherwise.

I barely managed a week of this fury before it began to take its toll. I was holding so much tension in my body that I kept getting stomach pains and a dull ache pulsed in my jaw where I was clenching it. I've never been quick to anger, it was just another way my insurmountable grief was making itself known. I'd got to the point where I could mostly take part in normal life again: I could see friends and family and they didn't leave worried for my wellbeing, I was performing well at work, my garden no longer looked like it had been abandoned. None of that made the nights any easier when I reached over to the other side of the bed and a cold fist gripped my heart when I felt empty sheets. I couldn't understand why she wasn't making herself known to me and her absence caused a deficit in my heart that I didn't know how to fill. It was no longer cavernous, but it wasn't shrinking quickly.

I signed up to see a therapist to help me the rest of the way through my grieving process and just making that decision made me feel a little lighter. I still couldn't bear to communicate with the ghosts who desperately wanted my attention but instead of screaming at them I quietly apologised and asked them to seek out someone else, at least for a time. I still saw the odd ghost while out and about, but at home they left me to my peace.

It was a mystery to me then as to why my belongings were still seemingly moving on their own. I was almost 100% confident that it wasn't me or the spirits. It became more and more blatant until I couldn't explain it away or laugh it off. Some of my food was also disappearing and I didn't remember eating it. I considered putting up cameras in case someone was coming in while I was out, but when I saw the prices I realised it wasn't possible for my bank account. On the day everything came to a head, I came home from work and dropped my keys into my key bowl. Only they didn't drop into the bowl, instead hitting the end table with a grating clatter. I really liked my key bowl, it was something I'd made myself during my brief pottery phase, so I went hunting around my house determined to find it. I found it in the fridge filled with spare batteries. Some of the anger I'd been trying to get over resurfaced then as I felt like I was going crazy, or someone or something was trying to make me think that. I ended up drinking a little too much to choke the anger down and dropping into a fitful sleep.

"GET UP, YOU'RE IN DANGER!"

I shot up in bed; ears ringing, heart racing and mind groggy. Erica was standing next to the bed, which cleared my mind and I immediately teared up and reached towards her.

She shook her head. "No time babe, run!"

I couldn't see any immediate danger but trusted her implicitly so I stood up and headed towards the bedroom door. I barely managed two steps before a hand grabbed my ankle and brought me crashing hard to the floor, its cracked nails leaving marks on my skin as it released its grip. I scooted away, unable to tear my eyes away in horror as a lanky man with grey-tinged skin began to crawl awkwardly out from under my bed. His joints popped and creaked like a rusty gate and as soon as his face emerged, he locked his eyes on mine with a terrible stare. As his right hand came out from underneath, I was distracted by a glint of light shining off something in his grip. When I realised it was a large knife, my brain thankfully chose flight instead of freeze.

I slammed the bedroom door and tipped a shelf in front of it to put as much distance between us as possible. I heard a clatter as he fell out of the room, skidding across the landing carpet. I'd reached the kitchen when he barrelled down the stairs at terrifying speed. He slashed towards my arm with the knife before he'd stopped so I didn't have time to move out of the way. My blood spattered in shocking drops across the floor but I felt numb looking at it. I grabbed the hot sauce I kept next to my stove and squirted some in his eyes as I backed away from him. I've never been so thankful that I like spicy food, and that chilli covers up my terrible cooking. While he screamed in pain I tore over to the front door. I slammed it behind me and tipped over the plant pot I kept next to the door in the hope of slowing him down.

I saw the door rattle a few moments later and rather than wait for him to find another exit I banged on my neighbour's door and screamed hysterically. It must have been nonsense that poured out of my mouth, but seeing my bloody arm he knew it was an emergency. He rang the police and let me inside to the relative safety of his house. The police arrived very quickly and as I watched them drag the intruder away through the window, he locked eyes with me again and I threw up on my neighbour's carpet. I'd never seen such pure evil before.

I found out afterwards that he'd been living in my house without my knowledge for weeks. It wasn't me or the spirits moving things and eating food, it was always him. I didn't recognise him initially, but it turned out I knew him. His real name was Neil, but I'd known him as 'Mystic Mick'. He was the first local fraud whose database I'd hacked into. His wife was a firm believer in the psychic arts and through my actions she came to find out he did not have the gift he claimed to. She made sure his clients knew this too, so he lost his wife and his business in one fell swoop and I was in the crosshairs of his blame. He'd been watching me for some time and once he realised I was now alone he moved into my attic. He learnt my schedule, ate my food, and moved my belongings around to make me think I was losing my mind. When this no longer sated his boiling hatred of me, it seems he decided I needed to be eliminated.

If I hadn't been so distracted by my grief and anger maybe I would have realised sooner, but the thought of him sharing my most intimate space is something I haven't been able to get over yet. I deep cleaned the house twice, thinking of everything he touched and tainted, but it never felt like enough so it's currently on the market. It will break my heart to lose the space I shared with Erica, but I just can't feel safe there anymore.

Speaking of Erica, as soon as the police left I rushed back into the house, hoping desperately she wasn't just a mirage. She wasn't. I just stared at her; I'd been desperate for this moment but now it was here I couldn't conjure the right words.

"I'm so sorry," she spoke, breaking the silence, "I thought if you saw me you'd never let go, because you can still communicate with me. I've only been poking my head in to see you occasionally, when I thought you wouldn't spot me. I've mostly been at my parents. I decided today that everyone was beginning to heal and I could move on, but when I came here to say goodbye I noticed that you were in danger. If I hadn't come when I did, I dread to think what might have happened!"

She placed her hand on my cheek. I couldn't feel her hand, so I closed my eyes and let the warm memory of her touch whisper across my cheek.

"I miss you," was all I managed to choke out through the salty mist of my tears, but I knew it was enough. She leant her head forward until it rested on mine, and I imagined the weight.

"We'll see each other again, I know it. I love you," she whispered.

Long after she moved on, in an awesome display of golden light, I stayed in place imagining her presence was still there. I pondered over the experience and realised I'm lucky because I got to say goodbye; I don't just have hope, I *know* there's something after this and I will see her again. I'm going to spend the rest of this mortal life giving others the chance to say goodbye too: that's what I'm here to do.

Author Bio

Angela started writing seriously during the pandemic lockdowns after taking part in ghost story writing courses. She generally writes short horror stories, much to the dismay of her Grandma!

So far Angela's work has appeared in anthologies from Sins of Time & Jolly Horror Press, and an upcoming anthology from Iridescent Words. Her flash fiction pieces have been published in an issue of ABFM magazine, and adapted for audio by The NoSleep Podcast. Some short stories and reviews can be found on her Vocal account.

Her personal Instagram @anginolan is also updated with her writing accomplishments.

Orion

by A.J. Herbert

They don't understand me. They don't want to try. All they see is someone who doesn't fit the outdated stereotype of what their boy should be.

Today I told them that I don't want to play football anymore. I don't enjoy it. I'm not sure I ever did. Maybe I was just going through the motions because it's what I thought I should like.

I'd reached a point where I realised that there were other things I'd prefer to do. Things I would actually enjoy! For example, I liked nothing more than sticking my Beats headphones on and immersing myself in beautiful melancholy for hours on end. Maybe in the future I'd be inspired enough to create similar heavenly sounds. If only I could actually sing.

My dad had other plans.

"You will play football. Every man in this family has played for their local team. It's not an option to quit."

"But what if I don't want to play anymore! Lots of boys at my school don't play. They do other things instead …"

"More fool them! I don't care about those other boys. My son is going to play football."

"You can't make me go. I'll refuse to play!"

"Do that, mister, and you will soon find yourself losing privileges. No TV, no going out with friends and NO SPOTIFY."

He leaves the worst until last, knowing that's what will hurt. I have a daily one-hour Spotify ritual where I discover old music. I know that screams of me just wanting to be cool, but I see it as catching up on things I wasn't able to experience the first time around.

"You can't do that; that's not fair. Just because I don't want to play football, I have to be punished?"

"When you live under my roof, you will do as I say. End of conversation."

I'm consumed with anger. I don't give myself time to hang around. I slam my feet into my boots and grab my parka as I storm out of the house. I scream "fuck you" on the way out, slamming the door with as much force as I can muster. That will send a clear message that I'm pissed. I know I'll probably have to deal with the consequences of my dramatic exit when I return…

My coat isn't fully zipped up until I'm halfway up the street, but I'm walking with intent. I have a place I go to when something like this happens. I follow the well-trodden path to my local park, head down and power walking.

I lift my head only when I see my special place: a small mound that gives me an open and entrancing view of the stars at night. As luck would have it, no-one else goes here at this time. I have the place to myself. It's my own personal haven.

The grass hasn't been cut for what feels like forever, so I force myself through the long reeds. Once at the top, I pick a spot and use my body to create a flat piece of earth. I lie down on my back, place myself into a comfortable position and focus my eyes on the night sky.

There is an infinite world out there, with infinite possibilities. And I can only see a small portion of them. I would rather be up there than down here.

***

I close my eyes and transport myself to one of these worlds. When I open them I'm on Bellatrix, a land I've visited often. I make my way through the dimming lights of the old town, tiptoeing down the cobbled streets this place is known for.

I'm heading towards Legato, an acoustic music bar I often go to.

I know I can lose myself in the feeling.

I order my usual (a Ginger Beer with extra ice) and plonk myself in the corner of the room. I exchange awkward hellos and polite nods with the locals. They have simply come to know me as the 'conflicted introvert'.

The theme of tonight is 'Female Warriors', leading to a set of stirring renditions of songs originally by Janis Joplin, Kate Bush, Joni Mitchell and numerous others. The emotion within the words, within the sounds, is enough to draw rivers from my eyes. I let it all out as subtly and quietly as I can. It's a release. A release I needed.

Once the music stops I sit there in silence, gathering my thoughts.

***

I'm back on Earth. I open my eyes and feel the cold sting of tears on the edges. I'm distracted by some rustling in a nearby tree and shoot a sharp look in the direction of the sound. I see the silhouette of a person.

"Who's there?" I call out.

I don't recognise the figure and before I can move towards them, they slither away in silence.

Thoughts start to flood my mind. Did they see me? Who was that? What were they doing here? In MY space!

It takes a few minutes before I feel ready to head home. When I arrive back, I unlock the front door, avoid any form of eye contact and head straight for my room.

I'm back playing football the next day.

***

At school, we're told we need to start thinking about our A-Level choices. I know what I want to do – I want to add drama to my options – but I know my folks will need some convincing. I spend the rest of the day psyching myself up for the difficult conversation.

"Mum, Dad, I've thought about my subjects and I'm pretty sure I want to do drama. Mr Smith said I have a talent that deserves to be explored. That's cool, right?"

My mum doesn't waste any time in responding, "Are you sure, Joshua? Isn't that a bit of a pointless subject?"

Dad chimes in: "Yeah, you'll never get a decent job with a subject like that. And it'll be full of nancy-boys."

"Nigel, there's no need for language like that. That's the same profession your beloved Natalie

Portman is in."

I wonder if talking about my other choices would sway their opinion.

"I'm doing English lit and sociology as well."

Mum hesitates before responding, "What about business studies or something like that? Just in case you need a career choice to fall back on. You like business studies, don't you?"

"It's alright, I guess. Not sure a career in business thrills me though."

"I'll tell you what: drop sociology and do business studies instead. Then you can do drama," she offers.

"Uurgh."

We find ourselves enveloped in a conversation that simply runs in circles. This seems to happen a lot. Any time I'm heading in a direction that they don't want me to go in, we end up playing this verbal game of musical chairs. Except I never get to sit on the final chair. They are persistent and stubborn. They never back down. And I don't yet have the inner strength to say 'No, I will do what I want to do. I am my own person.' In the end their persistence always pays off and I afford them another opportunity to re-route the next decision.

This time is no different. I see I'm not going to

win. After about an hour or so I reluctantly agree to their compromise.

***

Later that night I'm back on my spot on the mound. I need to zone out, lose myself in my thoughts. I need to be somewhere else. With the extra preparation time afforded by not storming out, I've brought my favourite beanie hat and matching gloves. The November wind is a bit nippy, and I'm immediately thankful for the extras.

I close my eyes and transport myself to Meissa. The lights are shining as bright as the sun and the atmosphere is buzzing. As I walk through the busy streets, my gaze is enticed by a neon-bright sign with the word 'Tragicom' sharply displayed. As I approach the entrance, I see that they are putting on a production of 'Angels in America'. I casually walk over to the box office stand to see if there are any tickets left for tonight's show: there are. Someone dropped out at the last minute and there is a ticket in the second row. Yes please!

The ushers welcome me to my seat, and as the lights go down I am immersed in a world of hallucinated dreams, contrasted against the emotional reality of the AIDS epidemic. I see

81

myself in some of the characters on stage, although I know I will never have to go through the horrors they experienced. But still, I want to be up there with them.

The show ends to rapturous applause. The lights of the theatre almost blind me as the curtain falls.

There is only one word for how I feel: alive.

***

Back on the mound, the silhouette is there again. Only this time I can see more than a silhouette. They have a face! Every few seconds they are glancing over in my direction. Do they know me? Do I know them?

I think about saying 'hi' but as I sit up to let the word leave my mouth, they seem spooked and disappear into the darkness.

***

A couple of days later, I'm sat in the kitchen as my mum prepares dinner. The usual work talk fills any silence that may have been there. To say I am bored is an understatement. But suddenly the conversation turns to me. I don't know how it got there but it feels contrived.

"Martha across the road was asking me the other day: 'Why doesn't Josh have a girlfriend? I always see him with girls, but he's never going out with any of them.'"

My dad rushes in. "He just hasn't met the right girl yet. Ain't that right, Joshua?"

I'm panic-stricken. But I must respond as fast as is humanly possible, or else there will be more questions.

"Right, Dad."

His face contorts as if thoughts are flashing through his mind. "Why aren't you with any of them though?"

"We were friends first, Nigel. Although, I suppose, as much as boys and girls can really be friends."

"My girlfriends *are* just friends. I'm not interested in them in that way."

"Right," says my Mum nonchalantly.

"You're not a poof, are you?"

My dad deals the bigger blow. I wasn't prepared for this next question, which was accompanied by a reserved sort of fear.

"Nigel, what have I said about that sort of language!" Mum objects.

"Hmmph. It was a perfectly fine word twenty years ago."

I avoid answering the question and let an uncomfortable silence fall upon the room. To break it I tell them I have homework to do and retreat to my room. As I close the door, my heart is beating faster than when Mr Pool makes us run laps in cross country. Faster than when I see Adam Jones in the school hallway and I try my best to be subtle and to not be consumed by his looks. The first tear drops the second I collapse onto the bed.

***

That night on the mound, I take myself to the land of Betelgeuse. Of all the places I take myself to, this has to be one of my favourites. It is by far the most diverse, populated with an array of different beings, many of which you would class as being other-worldly. And I always get the impression that despite this diversity, each and every being in this land would give the same helping hand to even their most hated enemies.

I head to the town square and find a free bench to perch on. My favourite thing to do in Betelgeuse is to just observe. It's at the point of the day where the shops close, and the restaurants and bars open. The smiles, handshakes and laughter are infectious, and I find myself greeting many of the passersby. Many of the locals have seen me before and their faces light up as they clock me. I am content and the Cheshire Cat grin I put on display tells them that.

I watch all the little groups settle at their tables and relax for the evening. I head over to the dessert van and order myself two scoops of ice cream. I don't care if it's cold. There's actually something very cool about eating ice cream when my nose has turned the same shade of red as the strawberry flavour. I'm immediately drawn in by some of the unique choices they have to offer. Today I plump for a scoop of tiramisu and a scoop of pea and mint. I enjoy my cone whilst losing myself in my surroundings.

***

I return from Betelgeuse calmed. But almost immediately I jump from my spot. The silhouette is no longer a silhouette. There is a full person standing directly in front of me.

It's the beanie I spot first, emblazoned with one of Keith Haring's most recognisable images. I'd learned about the artist during one of my internet wormhole sessions. I'd had many of those lately, where I'd sought to secretly teach myself about queer history. As part of this education, I'd made sure to learn exactly how I could remove any trace of the research. At the point where I found out that Keith died of AIDS, I'd felt a sharp pang of pain in my chest.

Below the beanie a small tuft of purple hair is poking out. I can't help looking this stranger up and down, immediately intrigued by their androgynous style. The remainder of the outfit comprises of rainbow branded Vans and mauve infused dungarees that match gloriously with the hair, whilst partially hiding a T-Shirt with the band Haim on it.

"Hi," the stranger says to me.

"Errrr. Hi."

"Sooo I see that you come here often. Well, I say often but I'm here every night, so not as often as me."

"Errrm okay."

"Sorry, I can be a rambler. My name is Aspen, they/them pronouns. And you are?"

"Joshua. He/him. Aspen's an unusual name. I don't think I know anyone with that name."

"Yeah, it's the name I chose for myself. My parents won't call me it, but my friends do. I love reading nature books and it's a type of tree. And trees are cool, so, Aspen!"

"Why won't they call you it?"

"It's not the name they gave me. That name means nothing to me. I hated it. But they can't let go of it."

"Oh. Why can't they let go of it?"

"Do you only ask questions when talking to other people?"

"Sorry. I guess so."

"No need to apologise. I'm just giving them time to get used to it. I'll tell you though, I deserve a 'Patience of the Year' award or something for waiting for them to get on board!"

"Ha."

"So, I think I've seen you at school. You're friends with Erica and Annie, right? I like them; they're cool."

They know me from school?! I try to hide my immediate guilt, as I can't return the favour.

"Yeah. They're the best."

"What brings you up here, alone, then? Instead of with them?"

"I just come here when I need time to think."

"I hear you. I noticed that you seem to go somewhere when you're here. Where do you go?"

"What do you mean?"

"It's like you're physically here but your mind isn't. Like you're in a dream or something."

It both concerns and intrigues me to hear Aspen pick up on my trips.

"I escape, I guess. I go to places where I feel comfortable. To feel more like me. Why do you come here?"

"Same really. I like to be with myself and get lost in my own thoughts. How old are you?"

"Sixteen."

"Aww, a baby. I'm eighteen. Anyway, it's been nice to officially meet you, Joshua. I need to head back now. Got an early start tomorrow. I'll see you around though?"

"Sure. Nice to meet you too."

"Awesome. Catch you later."

After a few minutes I head back home, avoid any unwanted interactions with my parents and sneak off to bed.

***

On my next visit to the mound, I find Aspen waiting for me. Their face immediately lifts into a gleeful expression as they spot me. As I approach them, they make room beside them and usher me onto a makeshift seat of flattened grass, soft and bouncy to the touch owing to its overgrown length.

"Hey, Joshua."

"Hey."

"Good day?"

"It was alright I suppose. I'm not really a fan

of school. I'm surprised I don't see you at school actually."

"Different circles and all that. To be honest, I like to keep myself to myself at school. Fade into the background, like. I find it makes things easier."

"Easier?"

"Yeah, easier. You ever heard of the term non-binary?"

"I think so."

"That's me: I don't identify as either female or male. I don't really mention it at school. I tend to hide in the shadows, you know, to stay off radar from those idiots who just won't understand …"

"Okay."

"Anyway, tell me more about you?"

"What do you want to know?"

"Anything you feel comfortable sharing, I guess. You seem like you're figuring stuff out yourself."

"Errrr. I guess I'm binary."

Aspen smirks and nudges me on the arm. "You don't say. It's okay, I accept you. Some of my best friends are binary."

I feel the urge to reveal my own hidden identity. I've never told anyone before, but I get the distinct impression that Aspen is giving me the hint to go for it. I take one of those gulps you take when it's really obvious you're trying to be subtle with it, but in the end it draws the attention of everyone in the room. I can do it. I hear the words in my head before I say them.

"Well, err, I'm pretty sure I like boys."

There. I've said it. I can't believe that I've revealed my biggest secret to a person I barely know. But maybe it's better that way. Less pressure. A huge wave of relief pours over every inch of my body. I have to physically stop myself from crying, instead catching my breath in the most un-subtle way imaginable.

With an arch of the eyebrows Aspen responds with, "Pretty sure?"

"Okay, I know I like boys. I think about them all the time. I tried not to. I tried to push it as far to the back of my mind as I could, but I can't help it."

"You like what you like. Ain't nothing wrong with that now is there?"

"I guess not."

"Am I the first person you told?"

"Yes."

"Oh, how wonderful. Well I'm honoured." Aspen lifts themself to their feet and bows as if I were royalty. They reach out their hand to me and lift me up off the ground. "Charmed."

Even with the cold air thrashing against my face, I am distinctly aware that I'm blushing.

"Always remember though, there's no rush to tell anyone. You've got a whole lifetime ahead of you to do that. Always take as much time as you need."

"I guess. Although I don't think I'll ever tell my parents."

"Oh. How come?"

"My folks have an idea of what they want their son to be. I just don't think I'm it."

"That sucks. When I told my parents about me, they were just confused. For a long time. The term non-binary is new to them. Sometimes I feel like they can only live in this world where there are boys and girls and nothing else. They're getting there but I guess it just takes time."

"Really?"

"Totally. The way I see it is this: they had an expectation of who I would become but I haven't become that person, so now they have to re-adjust that idea. I get that must be hard for them, although sometimes it does feel like they're making it all about them."

"Yeah, my parents are a bit like that. If I do

anything different from the expected, it's an argument."

"But you stand up for yourself, right?"

"Not really. I tend to just give in. Storm out. Come here."

"Oh Joshua. I can see I have much to teach you."

"Teach me?"

"Yeah, I need to introduce you to the queer world!"

"I'm not sure I'm ready for that. Yet."

"We'll take it slow. I promise."

Before we head home, Aspen makes sure to learn the names of all the boys I'm attracted to at school.

"I won't tell anyone. Cross my heart and all that stuff. I find it helps to embrace the parts of you that are kept hidden. Even if it's only in the presence of moi! I am judging you for Adam Jones though. What an absolute wanker."

"Ha. I think that's what I like about him."

My walk home is at a deliberately slower pace than normal. I want to take in the night air without the weight of the world on my shoulders. I realise halfway back that I don't remember the last time I came to the mound and didn't transport myself to another world. I didn't need it today. I am struck with a mixture of fear and excitement. These worlds are my solace, they are my escape. But maybe by escaping, I am failing to deal with the problems in my real life.

I wonder if I will ever need to visit my other worlds again.

***

At school the next day, I ask if I can be excused during a particularly uninspiring religious education lesson. My plan is to spend a good twenty minutes reading a copy of 'Angels in America'. I'd found it in one of those old-fashioned telephone box libraries, allowing me the readers' anonymity that I craved.

As I'm about to approach the toilets, however, I suddenly feel my body being pulled in another direction.

"I thought I saw you walk past," Aspen says as they loosen their grip, "I'm on a free period. Come with me, I wanted to show you something."

We head to the school library in a sort of walk-run and when we arrive Aspen takes me over to a new display in the fiction section.

"This is so cool. Look, they've created an LGBTQIA+ section. And it's not even Pride month!"

Immediately aware that I am in a public space, my eyes dart around to make sure no-one I know can see me. Once I've given myself the all-clear I take a closer look at this new display. I see all of the Alice Oseman and Becky Albertelli books I've been wanting to read for ages. I've been too scared to check them out for fear that the computer system would be leaked to the whole school, all to force an unwanted outing.

"I figured you wouldn't want to check them out, but I have an offer for you: if you pick a couple of books you want to read, we'll check them out on my card. We can make it like a weekly thing."

"Really?"

"Yeah, knock yourself out. You can keep them at mine if you don't want to take them home. I don't mind you reading them when we sit in the park."

"Thank you. This is so awesome." I go straight for all four volumes of Heartstopper and then realise they make quite a large pile when stacked together.

"Don't worry. I've got enough room in my bag for them. Give them here."

***

On our next trip to the mound, I storm through all four books in one sitting. I've never turned pages so fast. On multiple occasions I catch myself before tears start to fall from my eyes. Here in print is someone. Just. Like. Me.

Over the next few weeks, our arrangement allows me to explore all of the books I'd been eyeing up. I also introduce myself to the works of Oscar Wilde, Juno Dawson and Armistead Maupin. I wanted a varied mix and my fleeting journeys into the worlds of these authors allowed me to feel more immersed into queer culture. Occasionally Aspen reads them too and then our evening catch ups become something of an impromptu book club.

***

One weekend, we arrange to meet at the mound at 3pm. I am slightly nervous at the thought of breaking our school / evening meet-up cycle.

I'm also a little surprised that my parents don't question where I am going, what I am doing or who with. I'm never busy at this time. Maybe they think I'm going to do some regular teenager stuff, with regular teenagers, their minds immediately put at ease at the thought of some normality. What if they think I'm going to meet a girl and they don't want to be too over-bearing?

I quickly banish these thoughts from my mind. They will only cause me to dwell on my situation and not be in the moment.

As per usual, Aspen arrives in the park before me, and I quickly get the sense that they are up to something.

"Don't sit down. We're not staying here."

"We're not?"

"Nope. I've got somewhere to take you."

"Oh. Okay. I can't be out too late though."

"Don't worry, this will only be an introduction."

"An introduction to what?"

"You'll see."

***

Aspen leads us to the nearest bus stop and buys two tickets to somewhere I don't recognise the name of. We don't talk much on the ride, but Aspen seems to sense my anxiety and grabs my clammy hand.

It's clear where we're going as the barrage of rainbow and progress pride flags come into my line of sight.

"You ever been to a queer space before?"

"Errr no. I've never been brave enough to even think about that."

"Do you want to?"

"Maybe."

"I'll be here to support you," Aspen says.

"Okay. I'm a little nervous."

"To be expected. But I can't tell you how great it is once you go. And in like a year's time, you'll wonder why it ever felt like such a big step in the first place. Trust me."

We exit the bus and head towards a building that seems to disappear amongst all of the others. The lights aren't as bright here, but the same flags protrude from the entrance. A sign in the doorway reads 'Pride Cafe'. I peek inside and my eyes are drawn to a small counter with packets of coffee beans sitting next to a box of badges. Some have the rainbow pride colours on them, others have patterns and colours I don't recognise. My eyes scan the room and I see shelves full of what look like board games and books.

"What is this place?"

"This is your introduction to the queer world." Aspen shakes my shoulders loose. "Relax, will you. Do you want to go first?"

I glance back through the window and in the middle of the room see groups of people engrossed in conversation, one group playing a game I assume they've taken from the surrounding shelves. They are not like the people at my school. They're dressed differently and some have hairstyles that would definitely not meet my school's standards.

I take a massive gulp and respond in a whisper, "Sure."

Aspen opens the door and guides me in.

One of the people at the table turns around, sees Aspen, and immediately rises from their chair. "Aspen! So great to see you. How are you?"

"Hey, Ben. Good to see you too. I'm great, thanks."

"Good to hear it. And who's your friend here?"

Ben's enthusiastic smile immediately makes me feel more at ease.

"This is Joshua. But you have to be kind, he's a newbie."

"You know me, I wouldn't hurt a fly. Joshua, come and sit with us."

I look towards Aspen as if needing approval to accept Ben's invite.

"Go on, go ahead. I'm right with you, remember."

The others at the table make room for me and Aspen. I take my seat and let Aspen introduce me to everyone.

Ben re-ignites a conversation they must have

been having as we walked in. "We're just debating the merits of 'Happy Little Pill' by Troye Sivan. You know it, Joshua?"

"Know it? I love that song."

Aspen leans over and softly says to me, "Totally found your people, right?"

"Right."

As the conversation progresses, I find that I don't need to talk that much. I am just content with taking it all in, only responding when asked a question or asked for an opinion. Maybe down the line I will be the instigator of conversations. I just have to become more comfortable, like Aspen said, right?

We've been chatting for about an hour and the sun is beginning to set as Ben steers the conversation in another direction.

"Anyone up for a board game? You like playing them, Joshua?"

"Err, yeah, I guess."

We end up playing an old game I've never heard of called 'Master of Orion' and it doesn't take long before I am thinking of the worlds I take myself to. I haven't felt the urge to return to one of them recently. Maybe that's because I have some people in this world who will now be my solace, the outlet that I need.

Author Bio

A.J. (he/him) is an amateur writer, originally from the land of roundabouts and concrete cows; Milton Keynes, and now living in Northamptonshire.

He likes to read and write stories primarily from a queer perspective, partly to make up for the lack of these stories he had growing up.

A lifelong vegetarian and melancholy music-lover, he lives with his partner and their two pets.

Through the Darkness

by Claire Deacon

I'd never been particularly lucky in love, but meeting the woman of my dreams just after a pandemic swept the globe was a new low point, even for me.

It had been a year since my ex and I had split up, and, after wallowing in self-pity and regret for much of that time, I had come to the conclusion that it was time to move on. In fact, I decided to have a major life change and move out of London altogether. It had felt like a hip and exciting place when I first moved there in my twenties, but as I got older it just seemed more and more crowded and claustrophobic. Now that I'd hit thirty, I was ready for something new.

I'd been working at the head office of a conservation charity for several years and when an opportunity came up to move out of London, and get trained up working directly on one of our rural sites in the Midlands, I jumped at the chance. There were all manner of beautiful little villages near the site and after a whistlestop tour of them, I fell in love with one in particular.

I completed my bold move to the sleepy village of Upsworth, where I didn't know a soul, just before the first coronavirus lockdown was announced. Suddenly, it didn't seem like such a stellar idea after all. Now I couldn't hop on the train to go and visit my old friends in London, or get to know new people nearby, because everyone was only allowed to leave their house once a day to exercise. My employer immediately put me on furlough, and while in theory being paid to sit at home and do nothing sounded like an ideal scenario, in reality my days were filled with a boring, lonely tedium. I spent most of my time moping around my house listening to my favourite rock band, Witch Queen, and attempting to improve my poor guitar skills.

My one point of human contact were the delivery drivers who brought my groceries from the nearest supermarket. But today my friend (as I'd come to think of her), Barbara, had bad news.

"Sorry," she explained, looking like she'd had to give this speech already several times today and was expecting me to shout at her, "we're absolutely cleared out of several of your requested items. Including loo roll. It's like gold dust at the minute."

Crap, what was I going to do? I'd run out that morning. My only hope was that the small village shop might have some of the vital resource. I'd walked past it several times but had never been inside – it looked like today was going to be the day.

It was so still when I headed outside later that day, with the calls of birds the only sound and no cars on the roads. I caught the scent of flowers from carefully tended gardens and felt the glow of the setting sun on my face, and I started to feel almost peaceful. This was what I had left London for. Okay, not the pandemic part, but if you ignored that for a moment then it felt like all was right with the world.

Soon enough I arrived at the shop. I prepared myself for disappointment as I turned the corner into the toiletries section, resigning myself to having to google the awful sentence 'toilet paper alternatives' later that evening, but fortune must have been smiling on me because there on the nearly empty shelf were two packs of loo roll. I grabbed one and hugged it tight to my chest. "Thank you," I mouthed skyward.

I didn't desperately need anything else, but since I was already there I picked up a family-size bar of chocolate, a huge tub of ice cream and a six-pack of canned cocktails – my lockdown guilty pleasure. I didn't stop to think about how indulgent these extras looked until I plonked them down on the shop counter, then looked up into the eyes of an absolutely gorgeous woman.

"Somebody's got a fun night planned," she said with a raise of her eyebrow.

I had no doubt I was blushing a deep shade of crimson. Ruby, as her name tag identified her, looked about my age. Her afro hair was dyed a vivid blue and her facemask had small silver skulls on that glinted against her dark brown skin. The skulls, and the amount of eyeliner she wore, led me to believe she was a fellow rock music fan – or that she at least liked the aesthetic. I have always had a weakness for alternative women and it seemed too good to be true that there could be two of us in this tiny village. I was still attempting to form a witty comeback when she saved me from my embarrassment.

"I'm only kidding. We all have to find our enjoyment wherever we can at the moment, right? That'll be ten pounds, please."

I paid and packed my items into a bag.

"Oh, let me give you this." She handed me a leaflet. "From tomorrow we're trialling a new delivery service, where these cute little robots will bring your shopping straight to your door. All you have to do is download the Roam-bot app and you'll get ten percent off your first order."

I couldn't help but think I'd rather do my shopping here in person on the off-chance I got to see Ruby again, but that probably wasn't the responsible thing to do when we were all being asked to stay at home as much as possible to stop the spread of a deadly virus. Besides, delivery robots did sound pretty cool.

I was aware a queue was forming behind me so although I wanted to stay and chat to Ruby for longer (ideally all day) I mumbled a "thank you" and turned to leave. Just as I did, I noticed a splash of colour against her dark outfit – she was wearing a rainbow-coloured bracelet.

I made my way out the door and tried to stop my heart from leaping. After all, rainbows had appeared everywhere since they'd become a symbol of hope and gratitude at the start of the pandemic. But planted in me now was hope of a different kind – the hope that the beautiful woman I'd just developed an instant crush on might, in actual fact, be queer.

***

After my excursion to the shop, my days went on pretty much as normal but with the added bonus of a warm glow and a smile whenever I thought about Ruby – which was, admittedly, quite a lot.

Immediately on getting home I had downloaded the Roam-bot app and checked out how it worked. It was very simple, just like ordering a takeaway really, but instead of a harassed delivery person turning up at your door it would be a friendly robot (at least, I imagined them as friendly. Who knows if they actually were).

I didn't order anything for a while because it felt a bit childish to order something I didn't need just for the joy of seeing a robot trundling down the street. Then I remembered it was my birthday coming up. I'm not usually one to make too much of a fuss about my birthday, but thinking about the way my London friends always used to insist on treating me to a cake and singing happy birthday made me miss them more than ever. So when the day arrived, after I'd opened their cards, all containing promises to come and visit me as soon as possible, I got on the Roam-bot app.

After adding the most decadent birthday cake available to my virtual basket and selecting my choice of music for the robot to play ('Happy birthday to you', naturally) I hesitated. There was an option to add a note to your order, which would be seen by the shop. I was sure that Ruby wasn't the only one who worked there, so it was a gamble, but in the end it felt like too good an opportunity to pass up.

"Hi Ruby, you served me the other day – I bought a load of comfort food and you said I must have a fun night planned. I just wanted to thank you for making me smile :) ~ Kate."

I deliberated for a while, wondering if it was too weird or if she simply wouldn't remember me at all. But I had added a profile picture to my account on the app, so maybe that would jog her memory? In a moment of uncharacteristic optimism, I pressed the order button.

I spent the next hour gazing out of my living room window, waiting for the robot to appear. I had just started to lazily strum a few chords on my guitar when my phone buzzed with a notification: 'Your delivery is on the way!'

I rushed to my front door and peered down the street. It wasn't long before I saw the robot and I couldn't help but grin like a kid. It was a sleek white pod about the size of a carry-on suitcase and it stopped every few metres to readjust its alignment or to let a dog go by, before getting up a short burst of speed. Finally it reached my door, the big eyes rendered on its display screen making it look like something out of an animé show. It came to a stop and I took a photo of it for posterity before entering the code that had flashed up on my phone onto a keypad on the lid.

The lid popped open, the first notes of 'Happy birthday to you' greeted me, and there in its innards was not just the cake I'd ordered, but two cans of my favourite cocktail and an envelope that had my name written on it in big, looping writing.

Puzzled, I took everything out and went to open the envelope. Had there been a mistake? Had someone else's order been put in with mine? Before I could investigate further, the robot closed its lid and started trundling off back down the street the way it had come.

"No, wait!" I called after it, but it was no use. It clearly knew where it wanted to go. With a shrug, I turned and carried my haul back indoors.

I set the delicious-looking cake down on my

kitchen counter and tore open the envelope. Inside was a birthday card featuring a picture of a duckling wearing a party hat. I smiled and opened it up to read the message.

'Happy Birthday Kate! At least, I'm assuming it's your birthday from the cake and the music. If not, happy … cake eating, I guess! Enjoy these cocktails on me. Hope to see you at the shop soon. Love, Ruby.'

I couldn't stop a massive grin spreading across my face. Not only did Ruby remember me, but she'd gone out of her way to cheer me up on my lockdown birthday. She was obviously a very kind person. Or could there be more to it than that? Could she be interested in me, too? No, don't be silly. My brain shut down that thought almost as soon as it formed. That would be far too much to hope for.

***

A few weeks later, the lockdown rules were relaxed slightly. Now you were allowed to meet one other person from outside your household outdoors as long as you stayed two metres apart. I wished I had someone local that I could meet up with. My mind occasionally flashed to Ruby, but we didn't know each other well enough for me to ask her to meet up outside the shop.

Instead, my visits there became more regular and my chats with Ruby at the till became longer. I deliberately visited at the end of the day when it tended to be quieter, so as not to hold up any other shoppers, and it was always hard to tear myself away from her when closing time came. She was interesting, funny and smart. I found myself thinking about her more and more.

I also started wearing jeans and eyeliner and straightening my hair again, rather than falling back on the sweatpants and ponytails I'd become accustomed to while stuck at home. I tried to tell myself that this sudden interest in my appearance had nothing to do with the possibility of seeing Ruby at the shop, but that was clearly a lie. Getting to see and talk to her was always a bright spot in my day and yes, I wanted her to think I was cute. Even if she could only see my face from the eyes up.

One morning I was in a particularly good mood as I walked to the shop. I'd had an email from work setting out a cautious plan for a few of us to return; or in my case, start. It was nerve-wracking, but exciting. Maybe my new life was finally going to start.

I hummed my favourite tune as I gathered my

shopping and gave Ruby a big smile when I handed her my basket at the till. She wouldn't be able to see it behind my mask, but I hoped she could at least see it in my eyes.

Her eyes crinkled adorably at the corners and her gaze lingered on the new band T-shirt I was wearing; I'd decided to treat myself to some Witch Queen merch for my birthday.

"I love your shirt," she said, "Witch Queen are the best."

She liked my favourite band? Could this woman get any more perfect?

"I was hoping to go to their concert later this year," I said, "but it's been postponed. Who knows when it'll go ahead now. Besides, I don't have anyone to go with."

I realised too late that this could sound self-pitying, but it was simply the truth. Most of my London friends were pop princesses and, while I loved them regardless, it did mean I usually went to see the heavier bands I liked alone.

"I'll go with you," she responded quickly, looking right into my eyes. I wasn't used to seeing Ruby look so serious. Most of the time she would joke around to make me smile, but right now there was an intense look on her face, possibly even nervousness, as if my reply really mattered to her. Was she offering to make it a date? I felt slightly faint at the possibility, but even though we'd both clearly enjoyed getting to know each other these last few weeks, in that moment I convinced myself she couldn't possibly mean that and to not make myself look like a fool by assuming that she did.

"Oh, that would be great, I'd love a gig buddy," I replied, keeping my tone neutral so as not to give away how my mind was racing.

I could immediately tell I'd said the wrong thing. Her gaze fell from me to the till and disappointment radiated from the slump of her shoulders.

"That'll be £10.95 please," she said in her most professional voice, as if I were just another customer. Maybe I was. Maybe my lack of confidence had just made me screw up whatever burgeoning thing we had. I tried to think of something to say to save the situation, but my brain wouldn't co-operate and before I knew it I was back outside, walking home in an early summer drizzle and cursing myself for being so clueless.

***

Over the next few days, I couldn't stop replaying our interaction in my head. I went through it back to front and upside down, analysing every part of it to figure out what I'd said wrong. In the end, the only conclusion I could come to was that Ruby had been offering to go with me to the concert as more than just a gig buddy and had taken my response as a rejection. I was such an idiot. I had seen the hope in her eyes, and I think some part of me knew that's what she had meant. If I was being completely honest with myself, it was fear that had stopped me from responding more authentically. I'd been devastated when my last relationship had ended and had grown a sort of protective shell to avoid feeling that pain again. But here I was, feeling pain of a different kind anyway, and wondering if Ruby might be worth the risk of opening myself up to someone again. That is, if I hadn't already blown my chance with her.

I decided to stop moping around and reinstate my evening walks, something I had let slip a bit. It was staying light much later now and when I walked through the village green there were small groups of people gathered together, enjoying picnics or just talking and laughing. It was a welcome sight after the months of isolation we'd all endured.

On a particularly beautiful Friday evening, I

was following my usual route round the green, lost in my own thoughts, when suddenly Ruby appeared before me as if conjured from my imagination. She was in running gear and keeping up a steady pace, eyes focused on the path ahead of her until she turned her head and saw me. Her expression shifted, and I tried not to overthink what the quirk of her lip might mean.

She came to a stop the requisite two metres away from me, pulling her headphones off and giving me a wave. She was slightly out of breath and sweat glistened on her forehead.

"Hi!" I said, stupidly thrilled to see her, "It's strange seeing you outside of the shop."

"Yes, turns out I exist in the real world too." She gave a small smile but it didn't have her usual spark.

I realised it was me who'd messed things up between us, so it was up to me to fix it. It was time to be brave and come out of my shell.

"So, I just wanted to say: once things are back to normal, or as close as they get to normal, if you wanted to go to a gig together, or get a drink or something, that would be … lovely. Like a date. Together. With me." I forced my mouth to stop making words. Hopefully she got the picture.

Her smile was back, and this time it reached her eyes.

"I'd love that, Kate."

"Cool. Awesome."

We stood there grinning at each other and it was the first time I'd been tempted to break the lockdown rules – in that instant there was nothing I wanted more than to reach out and wrap my arms around her. My skin was buzzing with the temptation, but I accepted I would have to wait a bit longer.

"It's a beautiful evening," I ventured, "we could sit down and chat for a bit, if you're not in a rush?"

"I'd love to. I enjoy our chats at the shop but there's some things I'd rather not discuss when my dad might walk in at any minute!" We sat down on the grass as close as we dared.

Ruby's dad owned the shop where she worked. I knew from our chats that she'd moved away to Birmingham (the nearest big city) for University and had decided to stay there once she'd finished her IT degree. She'd only come back to Upsworth when she got furloughed from her programming job, to help out at the shop.

"It must be tough living back home with your dad when you've been independent for so long."

"It has been a bit of a shock to the system, having to share my space. Sometimes I feel like I've reverted straight back to my angsty teenage years." She gave a wry smile. "But Dad's generally pretty chill. He only makes the occasional remark about me finding a nice girl to settle down with, and his epic cooking definitely makes up for the parental guilt trips! Besides, I think it would have been pretty lonely living alone through this damn lockdown. I don't know how you've done it."

"A heavy dose of rock music and an indecent amount of canned cocktails."

She laughed, her eyes crinkling at the corners. My heart skipped a beat.

"In all honesty, it hasn't been easy at times. But despite everything, I'm still glad I moved here. I have a good feeling about this place, and I've already met one or two awesome people." I gave her what I hoped was some meaningful eye contact. I've never been the best at flirting.

"Yeah, I've actually enjoyed being back in the village a lot more than I thought I would, even though I'd forgotten just how white it is round here." She laughed. "But it's nice to be able to walk outside and see trees, and to feel like I can breathe. A lot of my friends from Birmingham were starting to move away to start families, and to be honest city life was starting to feel a bit lonely."

I felt a spark of resonance at her words and tried not to read too much into them. Maybe she'd stay in the village once lockdown was over? In theory she could do her programming job from anywhere. But just because I had been ready for such a big move, didn't mean she would be. I knew from our discussions that it hadn't always been easy growing up as the only black, queer, alternative girl in the village and I was acutely aware that our experiences of village life may be very different. Still, something in her eyes gave me hope that one way or the other, when the world opened up again, she didn't want it to mean the end for us.

We talked and talked, about our families, friends, and our mutual love of Witch Queen and what their music meant to us. I discovered her favourite song of theirs was "Another fallen angel" and told her mine was "Hold me in the darkness". It was so easy to talk to her, I didn't realise that the light had started to fade from the sky until I noticed her shivering. That urge to hold her returned with a vengeance.

"I guess we should head home soon."

"Yeah, I guess." She sounded as reluctant as I felt. "But let's start making some plans, yeah? Even if we can't carry them out just yet, it's good to have things to look forward to."

"So, um, shall I give you my number?"

"Oh, I don't have my phone on me at the moment," she gestured to her running gear, "but I have an idea. Will you be at home tomorrow morning?"

"Yes, no wild parties planned."

"Okay, great. Keep an eye on your front door around ten." She gave me a wink, then stood up to leave. But instead of heading off she stood there looking at me for a second, seeming to glow with the last shreds of light in the sky behind her. I drank in the image. After a couple of seconds, she stretched her hand out towards me, fingers straining, and I did the same back. It was the closest we could get to touching for the time being and somehow it was enough. The air between our fingertips seemed to tingle and shimmer, or maybe it was that nearly-forgotten emotion I was feeling – happiness.

***

I'm not ashamed to admit that I was waiting by my front window from nine am the next day. I'd popped on a bit of lip gloss and eyeliner, just in case, even though I didn't know if Ruby was going to turn up in person. I knew that she usually worked at the shop on Saturday mornings, so I was intrigued to see what she had planned.

I was daydreaming about the plans we were going to make for when lockdown was finally over and the coronavirus was just a bad memory, when a familiar friend came into view. It was a Roam-bot – and it was headed for my house.

I hadn't ordered one, so Ruby must have sent me something. Either that or the robots had turned sentient already. I hoped it was the former.

I went out to meet it as it pulled up outside my door. As I did so, I got a text from Ruby that just contained a four digit code. I typed this into the robot's keypad and its lid popped open. As I lifted it up the guitar riff from my favourite Witch Queen song blasted out, much to the confusion of a passerby and his dog. I grinned and sang along as the lead singer's silky voice kicked in:

"Hold me in the darkness and I'll hold you in the light. We've been through hell and back but now the morning's in our sight."

I felt my eyes prick with tears. There couldn't

be a more appropriate song for what the world had been through over the last few months.

There weren't any bags inside the robot this time. I crouched down for a closer look, still singing, and found a torn-off piece of paper with a number scribbled on it: Ruby's phone number. I smiled, then laughed out loud when I saw her note on the back.

'P.S. Don't tell my dad I hacked the robot to play Witch Queen. These things aren't meant to sing anything heavier than happy birthday ;-)'

I closed the lid and watched the robot as it made its way back down the road. It reminded me of the birthday gift Ruby had sent me all those months ago, and the budding connection we'd formed since.

I headed back inside and composed a text to Ruby with a grin on my face, but my joy had a bittersweet edge to it. I didn't know when I'd get to hold her hand or kiss her. I knew I would wait as long as it took, but it still made me sad that we had to keep apart for now. The uncertainty of the future was an ever-present cloud, but as I thought about the beautiful, kind woman who had sent me her phone number in a robot, and about the songs that got me through the darkness, I realised that I had the one thing that made it bearable: I had hope.

Author Bio

Claire (she/her) has been writing for as long as she can remember and has had nineteen short stories published in various anthologies. She enjoys writing and reading about queer love and is a passionate believer in the importance of community.

Claire's other interests include crafting, boardgaming and going to as many gigs as possible. Claire lives in the Midlands where she helps to run bookish groups for the local queer community.

A Piece of Me, A Part of Her
By Rosie Richens

As a physicist I don't believe in destiny. Kismet is a load of crap. The universe is pretty rigidly deterministic from what I've learnt so far and most, if not all, of it is set by fundamental laws and the initial conditions of the Big Bang. That being said, why do I feel like someone played a cosmic joke on me today by making the last day of our A level exams the hottest day on record?

My best friend, Anne-Marie, and I finished our last exam today in the blazing forty degree heat. Now we are free. This evening we're driving to a swelteringly hot post-exam party at our friend Steph's house out in the sticks. She has a pool in her three acre back garden!

Anne-Marie has been working solidly all year towards her exams. I, on the other hand, have spent most of my time since Christmas procrastinating, re-watching Doctor Who episodes. Only in the last few weeks have I managed to set aside my Doctor Who obsession and focus on revising for my exams. I hope I've done enough to scrape the grades I need next year. My exams have gone well enough.

I can't believe we're finally at the finish line. I can feel the summer holidays stretching out in front of us, full of promise. Our last summer together … I've been deliberately trying not to think about that. Anne-Marie is most likely going to get into a Cambridge college to study Medicine like she's always wanted, and then? Well, I'm not sure if I will ever see her again. We've been best friends since primary school, but still. It happens. People drift apart. Especially when they go off to a university like Cambridge. A place like that changes people. And not always for the better. I could be losing my best friend at the end of this summer. And that thought fills me with absolute dread.

Full disclosure: I think I might be low key in love with Annie but she has no idea that I've had a crush on her for most of secondary school. Yeah, I know, I'm a total cliché – gay best friend in love with straight best friend in unrequited pining tragedy, but here I am living my best life!

The sound of Annie's car horn beeps insistently from right outside my house. I glance out the window and see her little green Fiesta waiting for me by the roadside. I give Annie a quick wave to let her know I'm on my way. I run my hands through my short blonde curls quickly to spruce them up a bit. I thunder downstairs and say a cursory goodnight to my parents who are watching a Netflix film in the living room.

"Mind how you go!" calls Mum as I head out the door. I exit the house quickly before she can drag out the pre-party cautionaries.

Annie is waiting in the car, grinning from ear to ear. She's looking hot, like a dressier version of Harley Quinn: red hair done up in bunches, red lip gloss, hot pants, knee high socks, platform boots. I on the other hand look like some kind of amphibian genetic reject by comparison in one of my dad's short-sleeved shirts and jeans. I look like a boy, deliberately so, but Prince Charming I am not.

"Let's go!" I say as soon as I'm in the passenger seat. Annie revs up her car and we are gone.

Annie drives us down the back lanes to where the party is happening tonight at Steph's house. We laugh and joke and bounce off one another as we drive, feeling full of the joys of summer and freedom. I feel euphoric when Annie is happy like this. The whole world comes alive, the music on the car radio sounds better, the colours around us more vivid. When we are together, just being us – Annie and Jo – I feel truly alive, like the whole world is at our feet. King and Queen of all creation.

"I plan on drinking copious amounts of cheap alcohol tonight at Steph's party," I say, grinning. "What about you?"

Annie smiles a wry smile. "I may have one or two but I gotta keep myself sober. I'm driving home."

Her dimples are to die for when she talks. Be still my beating heart.

"And Sam might be there," she adds.

My heart sinks. Annie's hoping the boy she likes will be at Steph's house party tonight: Sam Corrigan. He's in our year, six foot tall and on the rugby team. Annie and Sam have been flirting on Insta DM's for the last couple of months, much to my dismay.

"So, is tonight the big night then?" I ask. I don't really want to know the answer to this question but I've got a best friend cover role to play here. "Are you finally going to ask him out?"

"Maybe," she says, eyes shining at the thought as she drives.

I don't think I'll be able to take it if she actually does ask him out.

"Let's see what happens, eh? The night and

the summer, my friend, are both young and so are we!" she says, grinning at me, keeping her eyes mostly on the road.

* * *

Steph lives in a large farmhouse out in the middle of nowhere; she's the only person in our year whose house could possibly fit the entire sixth form of our school comfortably. The party is in the barn out the back, set in the three acre garden along with the pool. I can see as we go through Steph's side gate it's been done up in the school's blue and yellow colours – cute! Music is pumping out the wide-open barn double doors and we can hear the first strains of 'Don't Delete the Kisses' by Wolf Alice. I can't see the pool house from here but I can hear the shrieks and splashes coming from behind the barn.

"I can't see Sam, can you?" asks Annie, scanning the crowd at the entrance.

I do a quick once over. Nope. Thank you, universe!

"Maybe he's inside?" I indicate the barn. "Let's go see."

We move to the edge of the crowd queuing to go inside the barn.

"Has Sam messaged you?" I ask her.

"Nope he's been ghosting me all day," Annie says in mild frustration.

At that moment Sam appears from the backdoor of Steph's house with his arm around Amber Walker's waist. Sam and Amber are quite obviously together. I turn around in time to see the look of incredulous hurt cross Annie's face. I don't know what to say to her. She marches towards them pulling me with her by the hand. Then she barges us past them both without saying a word.

"Annie, wait!" says Sam.

"Save it, Sam. We're done!" says Annie, turning her back on him.

Annie pulls us both through the back door of Steph's house and into the lounge. The music is muted in here and it's stiflingly hot. There's no one around except us. Annie is breathing hard. I think she's going to cry.

Instead, she says, "I need a bloody drink!"

***

Annie and I have been wandering around the stuffy house for a bit. After the Sam and Amber episode, I've offered for us to just go home but Annie is having none of it. She doesn't want Sam to mess up what is likely to be the last time we see many of our school friends. So we've done the rounds and spoken to quite a few people. I'm on my third drink of the evening. Not sure how much Annie's had. I keep trying to ask if she's okay, but she keeps saying she doesn't want to talk about it. So I just offer her my arms and she buries herself gladly in my embrace. I'm hoping I can give her comfort and support by physical means if she's not ready to talk.

We're sitting on the sofa in the lounge, arms around each other. She shifts the conversation onto me.

"So, my lovely Jo. My rock. My best mate ever. I've been wondering about something for a while now. And feel free to tell me it's none of my business, but … why have you never told me about any guys that you like?" she asks, looking round at me curiously from the crook of my elbow.

I sigh and ruffle my curls so I have time to frame an answer. Due to cunning skills of deflection I've always managed to dodge questions like this. In all our years as best mates I've never professed any interest in the opposite sex. But now I find I'm sick of hiding how I really feel. For once in my life, I want to be honest with her. I can feel myself starting to sweat uncomfortably. This could go horribly wrong. I look at her and think it's now or never. Time to come out to my best friend.

"I guess I'm just not into guys," I say quietly before I lose my nerve, scanning her face for a reaction.

Annie looks even more curious. "So … you're into girls then?" she asks, looking at me directly.

I can feel myself blushing. "Yeah, I guess so," I say, feeling like an imposter for some reason. I've never actually been with a girl so how do I know for sure? I look at Annie's lips, slightly parted, still a faint cherry red from her lip gloss. Made for kissing. She smells tantalisingly of coconut body butter. Yeah, I'm definitely gay.

I can see cogs whirring in Annie's mind. A smile splits her face.

"Jo, that's so cool. I did kinda wonder if you might be. Thank you for telling me. So, who do you have a crush on?"

"Well, I really like Zendaya, she's hot. And Sadie Sink. She's gorgeous—"

"What about at school? Anyone I know?" Annie asks insistently.

"Yeah, I Suppose I do. You know her actually. You know her really well—"

"Please don't say Amber Walker or I will literally kill you."

"No! God no, it's not Amber."

"So, who then?" She's trying to read me like she always does. I just want to tell her.

"Can't you tell?" I ask her in a husky whisper, taking hold of her hand. I'm trying to tell her with my eyes what my mouth refuses to say. Her eyes widen as she finally gets it.

"You mean ... me?" she asks in a small voice. No way back now.

"Yeah," I force myself to say. I feel like my chest has been opened up and my living, beating heart is on display for her to see and touch. Please be gentle with it.

"Oh. Um ... I don't quite know what to say," she says, taken aback.

What the hell was I thinking? I should have kept my stupid mouth shut. Now I've ruined everything. She's just ended things with Sam. I'm an idiot.

"It's okay," I say, pulling away, heart sore in my chest. "You don't have to say anything. It's probably the last thing you need to hear right now. I shouldn't have said anything."

"No, I'm glad you told me," she says earnestly, her hand resting on my arm. "I just need to process this."

I look up, searching her face, hoping to see

even the smallest spark of something. There's always been those small signs, lingering glances, hugs that go on longer than they should, hands that stray from where they are strictly decent and graze skin in a fleeting caress. Signs that this could be something more than friendship, but I've never had the courage to act on any of it. Like when she runs up behind me and hugs my back for no apparent reason. Or when she looks into my eyes sometimes when we're cuddling in her room, listening to music. I've always felt I was reading more into them than was actually there. Now I'm not so sure. At least she hasn't run away. There is (surprisingly) still hope.

"Right. I think we need a change of scenery," she says, obviously trying to lighten the mood. "Let's go dance!"

"Dance?" I protest, "You know I don't dance!"

"Awww, come on. Please? For me?" She's smiling and melting me again with those soulful eyes.

"For you? Yeah, okay," I murmur.

She pulls me up and I find myself being towed towards the barn again. I don't dance for good reason because I have absolutely no sense of rhythm. I manage to find every beat except the one I'm supposed to move on. This is going to be an absolute disaster.

Inside the barn the music is really loud. Annie confidently steers us towards the heaving mass of bodies. She's already in the groove, writhing her body around to the dance track playing. I stand awkwardly, feeling embarrassed. I feel like everyone's watching me. Sam Corrigan is giving me evils, standing with the crowd on the edge of the dancefloor.

Annie notices my lack of gyration.

"Come on!" she shouts in my ear.

"I can't. Don't know how to." I shrug. My limbs feel heavy and awkward and if I try to dance, I'll just look like a complete fool.

Annie stops dancing and comes to stand really close, facing me. She puts her arms around my shoulders and leans her body against mine. My arms come up to encircle her waist, automatically pulling her closer.

"Now follow my lead," she says in my ear, holding me so close I can feel the breath in her lungs.

She starts to move and I can feel her entire body next to mine. Our bodies move together as one to the beat of the music and I start to relax. It feels amazing, and something miraculous starts to happen: it's almost like we've melted into one being. Annie swings her hips next to mine, leading me into the rhythm and the movements. Her face is right there, eye-to-eye with me and she grins as we move together perfectly in time with the music.

"See you *can* dance!" she half shouts in my ear.

I can feel the pulsing beat in every part of my body. I wrap my arms around her and sway my body next to hers, feeling her rhythm. I completely lose track of time. With her, I can dance, maybe not well but I can feel the beat and it feels good: raw, primal. It feels human, to connect to her like this through the music. She's smiling at me, and I'm grinning back at her.

Then I feel her shift and change. Could that be desire I can see spark in her eyes? Her smile fades and she leans in and tentatively kisses me. Time stands still. Whole worlds are born and die in the time it takes for her lips to caress mine.

I step back, my breath catching in my throat. Time returns to normal and I can think again. But I don't know what to think; I'm so confused. I know I told her that I really like her, but is she just doing this because of Sam? Is she trying to make him jealous? Or is she drunk? What's going on here?

"What are you doing?" I ask her, my voice catching as I try to navigate the onslaught of emotions in my chest. My heart is a freight train heading for the buffers right now.

"Don't you want to?" she asks in a soft, low voice that makes my knees go weak.

I'm yearning for what I can see waiting for me in her eyes but I have to be sure she really wants this. That she won't regret this tomorrow.

"Yes! Obviously but … is this a good idea? I thought you needed time to process?" I ask.

Annie looks at me, appraisingly. She's reading me again. She can always read me. She can see how confused I am by this. "Come on."

She takes my hand and leads me off the dancefloor. Sam and those standing at the edge are staring at us in disbelief, mouths open. School DM's will be going wild not five minutes from now. I shrug sheepishly at Sam as I get towed past him again by a very determined Annie. We march out of the barn and into the twilight outside. It's getting dark and cooling off outside as Annie marches us all the way back to her car. She fishes her car keys out of her hip pocket enroute and blips it open when we're close.

"Get in," she commands.

I do as I'm told. When we are both in the car, she turns to me.

"Why wouldn't it be a good idea?" she asks.

I feel quite flustered. She's being very dominant right now, not a side I've seen much of before. I kinda like it …

"Well, this is all happening really fast. If we did anything tonight you might regret it and I might lose you as a friend," I say in response.

"Why would I regret it?" she asks, folding her arms across her chest.

"Because you're straight!" I blurt, as if it's obvious.

"How do you know I'm straight?" she asks stridently. "I don't know if I am or not because I've never been with a girl before. How am I supposed to know for sure if I've never tried it?"

"By now you'd kinda know if you were gay," I say, looking down at my lap.

"Some people don't. Some people don't work it out till they're much older. Surely it's up to me to decide when I'm ready? But even if I'm not gay, I might be bi. I've been curious about that for a while, about what it might be like with a girl and not a guy. And when you finally admitted you didn't like boys and that you liked me, well …" she pauses, looking me directly in the eye, "I thought, who better to explore that with than someone I trust completely? With you."

"But what if you don't like it and you feel all uncomfortable or awkward about it afterwards?" I ask. I need to know if she's considered this.

"Why would I feel awkward?" she asks, reaching out to touch me on the arm. "What's so awkward about trying something new for the first time? It's just answering a question I have about myself: do I just like guys or do I actually like girls or do I like both? Why would finding that out for sure make me feel awkward, or uncomfortable?"

"I-I don't know but … you may feel differently tomorrow. After all, you've just ended things with Sam …" I say, not unreasonably.

"Eh well." She shrugs nonchalantly. "He was hot but he was a bit, you know, stereotypical chad to be honest. Not much going on up top or not that he showed me anyways. You and I have way more fun together."

She looks at me with a wicked glint in her eye. I feel warmth creep into my body from that look.

"I will always want to be around you, Jo,"

Annie says, kneading my arm, her mischievous eyes full of promise.

My knees feel weak.

"No matter what. We've got three months till the end of the summer, then we're off to university. Why not spend those weeks having a summer romance with your best friend?"

And when she puts it like that, I can't think of a good reason not to and lots of tantalising reasons why we should. I lean into the touch, moving closer, looking deep into her renegade eyes.

"Are you sure?" I ask, reaching up and pushing a stray lock of auburn hair behind her ears. "I don't want to risk losing you even if we are going off to uni in the Autumn."

For an answer she leans in with smouldering eyes and kisses me. Electric sparks fly, my whole being seems focused where our lips meet. Everything else is lost. It feels right. It feels genuine. Like this could be the start of something amazing. We part slowly, reluctantly.

"So, what now?" I ask her, breathless.

"So … now I'm going to take you home so we can watch Doctor Who and make out." she replies in a low, sultry voice.

My heart lurches. I've been in her room loads

of times and always wondered about what it would be like to start kissing her. Butterflies have settled in my abdomen. I try to divert myself from thinking about that or I'll panic and make a run for it.

"You're not into Doctor Who though."

She's never shown the slightest interest in my obsession before now.

"Well, I'm far more interested in the 'making out with you' bit of the evening, but I find I'm in the mood tonight to try new things." she says, eyes dancing. She starts her car's engine and puts it into reverse gear.

"Right. Okay. Well, let's go!" I say, flustered. "Though you really should give Doctor Who a chance. I think you might like it …"

I'm rambling. My whole world just got turned upside down in a really marvellous way and the summer ahead seems even more appealing than it did before, especially if it's spent exploring whatever this is we've just found. I can't wait to see if all the pieces of this particular human jigsaw puzzle fit together. I don't even think to ask her if she is sober enough to drive.

It's heading towards full darkness on the way home from Steph's. There's no street lighting; the car's headlights are on but we can't see very far ahead in the gloom. We're both a little muzzy headed from the alcohol and loud music at the party and we're both very distracted by the fact we've just opened up a whole new vista to our relationship. I can't stop myself from reaching out to touch her as she's driving.

Twice she has to tell me to stop because she can't concentrate, but I'm not really listening. I'm whispering sweet nothings in her ear – or trying to. That's why she doesn't see the oncoming car.

***

I surface into the real world slowly, like a diver coming up from the deep. My eyes are closed, my breathing quiet. There's light above me and the noises of people moving about, picking things up and putting them down again in a quiet symphony of mundane sound. I open my eyes a crack. I see doctors and nurses moving about the recovery room. I move my head slowly to look at the gurney beside mine and I see Annie lying there. Reality crashes back into my brain.

"Excuse me," I croak out to one of the nurses near my bed. "Is she okay?"

The nurse comes over with a smile.

"Hello, Joanne, how do you feel?"

"I'm alright. Is Annie okay? How did the

surgery go?"

I got away with cuts and bruises from the crash three months ago. The other driver was in a big Mercedes 4x4 so he was perfectly okay, whereas Annie in the driver's seat of her little Ford Fiesta didn't stand a chance. She had a ruptured spleen and one of her kidneys got damaged by the impact. Then the other kidney stopped working under the strain. This huge black hole of guilt swallowed me when I found out and I made a pact with the universe right then that somehow I would make this right.

Annie woke up a few days after the crash but had no memory of what transpired for the whole night of the party. She couldn't remember me telling her I liked girls and that I had a crush on her. She couldn't remember our kiss on the dancefloor. I had to tell her about Sam and Amber Walker, but I couldn't find the words to tell her about what went on between us that night. Her blood alcohol test came back showing that she was under the limit. So it must have been me distracting her that caused the crash. And I had to live with that eating me up for weeks until I found a way to make amends.

It's been three months of innumerable tests and procedures for me to check both my kidneys are in good working order before I could donate one to Anne-Marie. It's taken many tearful arguments and discussions between Annie's mum and dad, myself and my parents to get to this point. Lots of psychological assessments as well to ensure we all knew that there were no guarantees for either of us. Through it all the only thing driving me was my desire to make sure Annie was alright. That I would make this right and then maybe Annie would remember and we could be together again. Stupid vain hope. That's not how the universe works.

"She's fine," the nurse says gently. "The surgery went well. She has your healthy kidney now. We'll be monitoring her closely for the next few days. For now, you both need to rest."

As if those words give me permission to relax, I close my eyes in relief. Sleep starts to reclaim me. I can't keep myself awake now I know she is going to be okay ... My Annie.

***

"Jo? Jo! Are you awake?"

Annie. My eyes flutter open and I look across at her. She's crying and smiling at the same time. Probably in relief. We're still in the recovery room. I've no idea how much time has passed but it can't have been very long. Unsurprisingly now when I move there is a dull ache in my lower back. I try to stay still and just rest. Annie wants to talk, so I let her.

"I've been waiting for you to wake up. The doctors say the surgery went really well and your kidney – my new kidney – is starting to work. It's early days but all the signs are really good! And I need to say this to you again: thank you, Jo."

The words come out like they are being pulled from deep inside her, like she *has* to say these things to me, like her life or mine might depend on it.

"Thank you for being you and for being my best friend. I can't believe how lucky I am to have someone like you in my life. You are the most amazing person I've ever met!"

She's still crying. I must admit I feel quite unsteady too.

"Jo – I remember!" she says, wonder and amazement in her voice. "I remember now!"

Her words are a lightning bolt in my brain.

"I remember us dancing and kissing at the party the night of the crash. I remember all the things you said to me. That you have feelings for me. I remember us!"

I really don't understand how this all fits together. Karma DOESN'T exist! Right? But let's not forget the massive coincidence that I just happened to be a tissue match for her. A coincidence like that doesn't just happen, does it? Why does this feel like fate, like I've just got my reward for giving Annie my kidney? I'm welling up, a lump in my throat. Annie remembers us.

"The crash wasn't your fault. I should have been paying more attention to the road. Please don't blame yourself. And ... And I really do think I might have feelings for you too," she says, all wobbly and uncertain.

She's so adorable right now I just want to fold her into my arms and love her forever.

"Can we try again, please? I want to be with you."

"Yeah," I say thickly. "I want to be with you too. So much. I-I love you Annie." When else am I going to say it?

We reach out to each other across the space that separates us, despite the pain which stabs through the blanket of drugs we are both on. If it wasn't for all the drip lines and tubes snaking in and out of us – and the fact I've just had part of my body removed – I would be across this space and next to her faster than the speed of light. I have to content myself with just holding her hand.

I know now, looking at her, that everything is going to be okay. Because we fit together. The shape of her feelings matches the shape of my own. We have this shared experience that's bonded us before we have to go our separate ways. I'm content knowing whatever happens now, whatever the universe or karma has in store for us, whether we are together or not: a piece of me will always be a part of her.

Obsidian

by Jodie Neely

In a time lost to time

Throbbing forehead against dirt-ingrained fist, Ramuri keeps her eyes closed a few moments more.

Where loose tendrils of her dark hair touch her skin, they're damp.

Where grit aggravates her scalp, it itches.

Where pain pulses through her breaths, she wants to wince.

Yet she does not move. Not even when a miniscule fae creature drops from the sky, investigating her rent shoulder plate and the sticky gouge of her skin with needle-like teeth.

It's meant to be autumn, but it's so hot that the sun is making a sizzling plate of her back. The still, hot air makes breathing harder under the weight of her armour, let alone moving to displace the creature or her various other discomforts.

It's not just the heat though, or the pain, stopping her from moving and following the tantalising trickling sound of a nearby river. It's that she'll be damned if she takes the short, pain-filled hobble there and returns to find someone taking the credit for what she's done – not after all the trouble she went to.

She forces her eyelids open to turn a glare at the corpse's gigantic head.

Russet scales catching the light, its wide jaw hangs open to display tens of yellowed razors, a blackened forking tongue lolling out into the brown sun-burnt grass. The eye staring right back through her is glassy with death, but its iris remains as gold as the autumn leaves of the forest. Its other eye, invisible from her vantage point, did not fare so well in their fight; that one is a mess of crimson tissue where her knife tore into it – just after its teeth became more friendly with her shoulder than she liked. She doesn't know where her knife is now, but it saved her life when she needed it, and she has more important things to worry about.

After all, today this one almost had her. Good. And. Proper.

So, understandably, she wants something for her trouble. But how long until the corpse begins to smell of more than coppery blood and fusty reptilian scales? And her shoulder, too?

There's all the anticipation in the tracking, all the adrenaline of fierce battle, and all the triumph – the satisfaction – of slaying a dragon against the odds. They never tell the part where the hunter sits out in the middle of nowhere, wounded and waiting for some terrified townies to realise they can't hear the dragon roaring anymore – and for one or two braver fools to investigate ... to find her.

Glory counts for nothing with her, and although the coin isn't foremost in her thoughts, coin helps when you have nothing more than coppers in your pocket and the armour on your back. Damaged armour, at that. Coin also helps when you're travelling from one end of the world to the other in search of the ghosts of lost things.

Sliding her gaze over the dragon's head, down the cobbled road winding lazily through the sparse trees and rocky earth, Ramuri finally takes a sharp, deep breath and slips gently from her resting place on the great foreleg of the beast. Her scabbard rattles against its curved claws like a xylophone, and the fae creature flits from her shoulder, disgruntled.

Its ire is beneath her notice, because everything aches in protest as she lands with a stagger, sickness rising from her stomach into her throat. Good arm braced on her knees, she takes a few deep breaths, waiting for the initial wave to pass.

Tap, tap, tap.

As she leans over, the silver chain around her neck slips from beneath her breastplate, the little silver charm at the middle knocking against her chin. Even though she can't see it, she knows it well enough: a simple piece, well-crafted – and made for her.

An old adage floats into her mind: don't think too hard about things that can hurt you.

Too late. She's drifting – thinking of *her.*

Remembering a flash of violet eyes and hair so pale it's white rather than blonde; the plaited rope of it swaying, woven with silver beads and charms.

Remembering the beginning: a cold winter night, the grey stone city dusted with snow, and the bar packed with customers – because nobody wants to be caught in outlying areas as bitter winter sets in. The stranger with violet eyes picking her out from the crowd and offering her a smile so warm that it defied the bitter cold. The way she instantly liked her. More than liked her, actually – though she would not have admitted it.

Remembering return trips to the bar in following days and weeks. How familiar nods between them became small greetings, became small exchanges of words, and became talks over spiced wine until the bar closed. They exchanged tales from their journeys by the fire as blizzards raged. The dragon hunter spoke of winter forbidding long nights out in the wilderness on a trail; her acquaintance of how winter forbade travelling in her wooden caravan to trade self-forged silver trinkets and charms.

Remembering the first kiss. The heat, despite the snow and freezing rain as they said good night one early morning. And then, how they started not to say good night at all …

Remembering how the warmth between them stayed long past the first buds of spring on the trees. How, when the rickety wooden caravan painted in wildflowers and pulled by an old horse left town, it had two passengers rather than one. They went in search of dragons to slay, and wherever people required silver charms against life's ills.

Remembering dawn's soft light silhouetting her features amongst the knot of blankets. How, in a new day's light the silver charms in her hair burned pink, and how the coin-sized chunk of black obsidian in her right earlobe grew almost luminescent.

Remembering her own repeated warnings that dragon hunters have short lifespans: an occupational hazard. Who wants that kind of trouble and pain when there's enough to go around in the first place?

Remembering how her love told her she would rather lose her to death than walk away.

Remembering a smile so close and tender that it's all she could see. The way that smile threatened to rip her heart from her chest every time—

There's a sudden painful jolt in her shoulder. Ramuri woozily forces her eyes open, not having remembered closing them. Her injured arm wedged under her, she's lying on the forest floor, wondering how she got down there.

She never needed anyone until she had someone. And now, when she has never needed someone more, there is no-one. In the time they were together, it never crossed her mind that she would be the one left behind. Alone.

Shaking her head, she tries to dispel the clouds of memory and haziness lying about her, and begins to get to her feet again. It's more difficult than before.

She's barely gained her balance when there's a sound in the sun-crisped forest behind her. Something large. Something rustling over leaves at speed. Something scaly.

Before she can turn, a rush of air nearly knocks her flat again as it leaps over her: dark scales warping the light as it passes overhead. She catches herself, taking in the sight of it warily, her head so thick with inertia she can barely think straight.

It flaps its wings tentatively as it lands – surprisingly lightly – on its four taloned paws, sending leaves and dirt flying, its tail coiling as it whirls to face her; a grace that would be wondrous if it didn't have long and wicked-sharp claws at the end of each muscular leg, or wings tipped with black barbs, or teeth enough to bite clean through bones without blunting. If only it weren't a dragon.

Its scales catch and absorb the sunlight, and with its head raised every sculpted bone of its narrow face is cut out like a shadow, its nostrils flaring wide as it breathes her scent of blood and dead-dragon gore.

Then, she catches her breath.

Its otherwise perfect head is missing an ear.

What was it the forest hunters said they saw, on the day she lost everything? A black dragon: one eared. She wasn't fast enough to see it herself; late enough only to see the blood it left. But that's enough. She's sure this is the same creature: the one that devoured the woman she loved.

With a heavy arm, she draws her sword with a crystal-clear ringing.

The creature eyes her from its distance, as still as if made of stone, whilst she breathes heavy, the blade quivering in her hand. She can't keep it steady, no matter how hard she tries.

They're like that for several moments, before the sound of horses disturbs the forest behind her. She dares not take her eyes from the dragon.

"Get back!" Comes a shout some way behind, the horses' hooves scraping to a halt, the steeds whinnying disconcertedly. "This is Faction business!"

Factionmen. Makers of war weaponry for warrior queens, and for petty lords who have too much coin. She fails to see how it is their business at all.

When she opens her mouth, she can taste

blood. Her voice is hoarse and crackling, but she makes herself heard, "This is only the business of—"

Against her own judgement, in her clouded mind she makes that fatal mistake of trying to warn them back with a glance over her shoulder, the word 'revenge' dying before she can speak it, as she hears the distinctive sound of bows being drawn. Sees two Factionmen with arrows nocked and aimed at her chest.

The fatal mistake is that the distraction is all the dragon requires to pounce.

The ground reverberates as the beast lurches, and she sees the arrows flying loose, just as the strength of the dragon's head slams against her right side, scales rattling against her metallic armour. Lifted clear off the ground as it throws her sideways, her sword vanishes from her hand, and the earth greets her again some feet away with a thud.

Ears ringing, air knocked from her lungs, she doesn't have the breath to cry out as her injured shoulder sings with a blast of pain.

Looking up to see if the dragon is coming to eat her, her vision sways, blurs and tilts. It's not coming for her yet, but it's obvious the two Factionmen don't stand a chance. Much less her. The creature is fast, whipping and snapping its body as fluid as water: jaw clattering, claws slashing, wings tucked sleek against its ridged back.

Bracing herself inches from the ground, the world spinning, there's a dribble of blood forming a puddle beneath her. The bent-in shoulder plate around her wound is now digging into the flesh. Looking at it makes her head spin more. She doesn't lie to herself: it's not looking good.

She's struggling to her knees when the dragon fells the second Factionman, its great head swinging towards her.

As if distance can help, she begins shuffling backwards, leaves crunching beneath her.

Fixing her in its gaze, it pads leisurely, claws scrambling the earth. She's injured prey after all, and not going anywhere fast.

Beads of sweat break and roll across her forehead.

And just as she thinks she can't bear the pain of movement anymore, her hand grasps something cool and damp and crusted with blood: her lost knife. Now a last defence.

Hidden, she grasps the hilt in her fist, the sharp edge flat against her forearm, and forces herself to back up further as, every second, it gets closer.

She urges it silently, knife concealed.

Closer … Closer …

Slaying it would be the best outcome, but she'll settle for less.

Then it's a mere foot away, reptilian head lowering, its maw closing in.

For the first time, she truly notices the dragon's eyes.

And hesitates.

Because they're violet …

Ramuri trembles, first realising she's losing precious time, then realising that the dragon stares right back. That it doesn't attack. Doesn't so much as shift its heavily-fanged maw, nor raise a claw. It should have. She should be dead.

What is it doing? What is she doing?

But those eyes …

They're the same as those she stared into so many times: hoping and wishing, and praying to gods she didn't believe in, that she could look into them forever. The eyes that, every day since the last, she hoped she could look into again.

Impossibly possible ...

She hears herself sobbing, knife slipping from her grasp, forgotten. Body suddenly numb, she forgets the agony in her shoulder even as a shuddering breath wracks through her.

"Tanjya …" Whispered as tears leak into the blood and dirt caking her cheeks, the name almost choking her as she speaks it.

The dragon blinks, dipping its head ever-so. The movement dislodges a glistening silvery tear that was flickering in its eye and it runs down the obsidian scales of its angular face … *her* face. Tanjya's face.

Who knew that dragons could cry? Who knew that dragon hunters could cry for dragons?

Despite the tears, she smiles sadly to herself, unable to look away from that familiar violet gaze.

The woman she loves isn't dead, and though it leaves her with more questions than answers; though she doesn't know if, or how well, they can make it out of this; whether she'll survive her wounds, or they'll find a way to change Tanjya back; she knows now that the old adage is wrong. The truth is: thinking too hard about things that can hurt you, can sometimes bring you right back to them.

391 years later, at the end of the world

Some would call it ridiculous to keep an appointment at the end of the world.

It must be said that Elspeth Natoori is anything but ridiculous.

Keeping time is difficult with the sun slowly dying, bleeding redder in each rotation. That's what you get when the world's hero disappears halfway through their heroics, leaving a psychotic god to win the war. At any rate, Elspeth is there. Of course she is. Where she's concerned, her end of every bargain is carved in stone. '*Meet me at the pier*' was the agreement. It just isn't much of a pier anymore.

As if some large beast has chewed it, jagged chunks of walkway and balustrade are missing – leaving yawning great gaps – and the endmost six metres of the pier have disappeared into the ocean. The spear she brought with her stands bolt upright several feet behind her on the pier, wedged between two stationary gaps in the wooden planking; the silver bell tied under the spearhead jingling faintly in the wind on its red ribbon.

It doesn't bother Elspeth that the pier is rickety, that one false step could send her into icy waters, or that if she does end up in there some genus of unknown creature could make her its dinner. As she perches on a still-standing balustrade near the pier's new end, the wood croaking and whining, she hums an age-old melodious ditty about a weaver spinning fabric from starlight. The haunting melody gives her goosebumps. Or maybe it's just the cool wind needling her skin. Fat chance she will hear a minstrel sing it again soon. Perhaps ever. It's been two weeks since the world, as it was known, ended. The wounds are still raw and she keeps finding unexpected ones like that.

It's not just 'things' either. Treasure hunter, mercenary, Queen's guard … what is she now? Where is her place in this new world? At least the brine of the sea smells the same, as it breathes through the tight curls of her hair and deposits a stiff layer of salt against her skin.

Before she can consider humming something less maudlin, there's an electrical prickle on the wind. Three metres away, thin air converges, and a figure materialises from the feet up.

Wolf. He has a real name, known to his friends. He and Elspeth aren't friends.

It's a shame, she thinks, *that he failed to materialise above one of the pier's many breaks...*

Once his head finishes re-assembling, they exchange a scowl. It's irrelevant, but she notes he's paler than he was several weeks ago, his deep brown hair hangs lanker across his shoulders and his mouth is thinner – more disapproving.

"I already know," is her opening line.

"The hero isn't dead."

"Then what do you call *this*?" She gestures vaguely at, well, everything.

"Temporary mishap."

She scoffs, biting down abhorrent words. She doesn't want to linger here. "So if the hero isn't dead, is Bear alive too?"

An abrupt nod. "And taking it hard."

You think the rest of us aren't? "Fox?"

"That's why I still came. Despite … everything."

He uses the same world-encompassing gesture she used before, but she's focusing on his implication: that if not for Fox, he wouldn't have kept the meeting at all. Her eyes narrow.

"Fox went rogue," he continues, before she can respond further, "she ignored orders, infiltrated the enemy's northern camp, took down the commander there, then succumbed to injury. It threw their northern front into confusion, but…"

What a waste. She knows he's thinking likewise.

Elspeth gazes at the choppy waves, grinding her teeth. The rest of them aren't nothing, but Fox? She is – *was* – something else. Irreplaceable. If they had all disobeyed orders, maybe then ... But lost futures don't bear thinking about anymore. It can't be changed.

"That's all?"

"I have this."

She doesn't look, though tempted. "What is it?"

"Here, catch. You tell me."

It whistles as he tosses it in her direction. She snatches it easily from the sea air... then the air leaves her body.

"W-where did you get this?" Her words are snatched away under the thrashing waves and constant creaking.

"So, it *is* a relic?"

She hops backwards off the balustrade, eyes fixed on the smooth, opaque coin-sized black gem in her palm. "Obviously."

He glares at her. "You were as obsessed with relics as the late Queen. If anyone alive is going to know, it's you."

Elspeth rolls the piece between her fingers. "Almost sounds like a compliment."

"Not from me."

She almost grins. "You mentioned Fox. She had this when …?" She can't finish that sentence.

He nods slowly. "There was a false compartment in her metal leg."

"When did she lose—" she starts. "Actually, I don't want to know that. I want to know how she got this and why she didn't mention it."

"Fox had her share of secrets."

"Don't we all?"

"How do we harness its power?" he presses, impatiently.

A scoff. "It's probably not *that* kind of power. Do you really think that because 'it's a bit relic-y' it will be the same? That's like saying every animal with four legs is a horse. The relic our late Queen utilised for strength was a fluke find. We'd be lucky to find something similar. Even then, it wouldn't make a dent in this mess-of-a-world. You're clueless."

"I knew to bring it *here*." Wolf's arms fold neatly across his chest. "What does it do, then?"

Sighing, she hops sideways to another patch

of pier. "No idea. And before you ask: I don't know how to access it, or find out – and no, I'm not getting involved."

"How long will it take?"

"Didn't your ears form proper—"

CRACK.

Lightning smashes into the pebbled beach, shattering and spraying stone.

The flash is blinding and disorientating.

Near at hand, the little bell on her spear begins to thrash wildly in invisible gale-force winds. Cursing under her breath and lowering her arm from her eyes, Elspeth makes out shapes forming from the scorch marks and smoke.

"Go!" She yells to Wolf.

"The relic—!"

"Find me later!" She's already tucking it into an internal pocket in her vest; it's cool and lumpy against her skin.

She swears that, as he disperses into thin air, he's smirking. He knew she was bluffing – that the treasure hunter turned intellectual within her wouldn't be able to resist – but first, she has to escape the pier.

From the lightning crack, singe marks form into figures who swarm onto the pier's entryway like ants. They jostle and squawk in inhumanly high-pitched cries as the treacherous pier shakes, screeching in a cry of its own. Some fall in, but the rest are too focused on their prey to notice. They're just shadows of people, after all: everything human having been stripped away. Seeing them makes her skin prickle and her gorge rise. In that moment, she'd trade a lot for a scrap of Wolf's type of magic. To just dematerialise, instead of clawing for her life. Just once. Apart from that, of course, she reminds herself she wouldn't want to be like him at all; magic generally sits ill with her, in all its unexplainable peculiarity. She has always been much too grounded in the tangible.

Snatching her spear with its wild-ringing bell, Elspeth throws back her spear arm, leaning all the way back with her shoulder as the creatures gain the halfway mark of the pier.

She's not thinking about how close they are. She's thinking about trajectory, wind power, balance and force. Calculates it all in a second. And throws, with all her strength.

Not waiting to see if her throw hits its mark, she whirls on her heel and dashes toward the broken pier's end, listening to the spearhead bell jingle, even above the ruckus. A frenzy of squawks is her first good sign, a judder of the pier her second. Because the bell isn't an ordinary bell: made of a chemical type of science, it was always the get-out plan. Why would she put herself in danger without one?

As a second judder rocks the pier, she leaps out over the roiling dark waves, not thinking of what could be lurking in the depths.

The pier shatters in an explosion of splinters and singed shapes over her head as she falls.

She touches her hand to the relic's lump against her skin, gasping in a deep breath before plunging into the ocean.

***

The narrow cave smells of old seaweed. Soaked outer garments laid out on the dry rocks behind her, Elspeth shivers a little in her underlayers – but she won't risk a fire so close to the pier and she can't risk exposing her real lair. Not now she has the relic. She will just have to wait it out in shivering dampness before moving on.

She takes the stone from its hiding place, still able to make out its obsidian sheen even in poor light.

With it balled in her fist, Elspeth tries to keep moving – keep relatively warm – though she's also conscious of how exhausted her body is. As she finally slumps against one rocky wall, she tells herself it'll just be five minutes.

Then her eyes close, and she goes somewhere else.

***

I'm trying to pretend it's not goodbye.

I'm not fooling myself. I never did.

She's a solid shape beneath the blanket, even without her armour. In sleep, tendrils of dark hair tangle over her olive, weather-beaten skin; the silver charm necklace I made her gleaming at her throat.

I lean closer, intending to place a final kiss on her cheek, then think better of it.

Biting my lip and turning away, I catch my own reflection in the breastplate of her armour where it lies nearby in a cushion of green grass. Backlit by dawn, the light winks in my right earlobe's obsidian gem, but it's the look on my own face that catches me. I look physically pained – right down to the pits of my eyes.

I think I love her.

I don't think I'll ever truly know and I have nothing to compare her to. There just isn't enough time in the world for what we could have had.

Before I can change my mind again, I creep away into the morning. Away from the old wooden caravan that has been my home for a decade, and from the dragon hunter who looked at me like I mattered every day of our five full moons together.

I knew what she was the first time I saw her and knew it could never last – but of course, I let it happen anyway. And in the end, we were more alike than I thought; me and her …

But I shake all those thoughts away. It's all over. I have to let go.

I walk two miles down the dirt track leading towards the nearest village, then veer off into the forest at its outskirts. This forest stretches for miles and miles towards distant mountains. When I'm far enough inside not to see the roadway, I reach my thoughts out to the obsidian gem in my earlobe – mentally stretching as if with a muscle I haven't felt in years – and with a thought, tug.

Immediately it's like the sky begins to tremble, though it's all just inside my head. A reaction. Mentally tugging on the gem is like screaming "I'M HERE!" at the top of my lungs, through a megaphone on top of the world.

Then, sitting down on a nearby rock, I wait. I

spend that time trying not to think. Luckily, I don't wait long.

They warp in out of nowhere; three Faction handlers, looking alert and ready for a fight in their full, crested battle robes. When they see me sat there, a mere and meek human, they have the gall to look confused. It's my first clue that, in a decade, nothing has changed. I haven't touched the power in all that time because I knew it would call them down on my head, yet they expected to find me finally accepting this curse they put upon me.

"I saw that the bounty on my head has gone up for the first time in five years. Why the panic?"

They stare. They expected a lot of things. They didn't expect this.

"Well?"

The central one inclines her head: "Trouble North, for a client of ours. We need you to …"

Whatever else they have to say is meaningless. Because that's all Faction cares about; making weapons to make money. Same old story. All I needed to know.

This time, when I mentally reach for the obsidian gem, I let my whole being slip into it until it devours me.

The change is fast: skin stretching, senses

sharpening, form elongating in half a second. It's so fast that the central one is still talking when I snap my long dragon's body forward, my head slamming her backwards into the trees mid-word.

In a blink, I coil back on myself, out of reach from the others' blades, and let loose a roar so bone-chilling that I can feel non-existent hairs on the back of my scaly black neck. For miles, birds, animals and humans must quake.

I don't accept this curse Faction forced upon me, but I didn't say I wouldn't use it eventually by my own will.

One of the two Factionmen still cowers as I cease my roar. There's an opening there to lunge. And though my every fibre warns me against it, I do it anyway. I'm too at one with the instincts of the obsidian gem.

Trouble is, I don't see the other one coming until there's a silver blade by my head. A decade of inexperience shows.

I dip, but it's too late to back out completely and as the blade falls, I'm thinking of *her*: Ramuri.

Yet though there is pain, when the blade connects, I don't die.

I rebound slightly around some trees, then

look back, hissing as warm blood dribbles down my scaled face.

Only then do I realise what he was *really* going for. Not a death blow at all…

On the forest floor lies my right ear. In that ear is the obsidian gem.

A chill runs through me as I bound back towards them, but the one that slashed my ear off already has it and is warping faster than I can get there.

When I reach the spot, all that remains is crimson blood.

Without the mind touch of that obsidian gem … I try to connect, but it doesn't work; like without it, my body has forgotten what it should be.

I.

Can't.

Change.

Back.

I roar and roar until my dragon throat goes hoarse. I can't speak – I can't even cry.

And once again, I think of my dragon hunter and her shining armour, and how she might already be following those roars of mine …

I dash further into the forest.

I dive on towards who knows where and as I

flee, I hope that my dragon hunter doesn't miss me and my foolishness too harshly. I never told her my entire story because I thought I was protecting her – what if I've just gone and made it worse?

I hope that she forgets me. I would deserve that.

Even so, there is a part of me daring to wonder that maybe, one day, I can find a way back to her and find out what we might have.

***

Elspeth wakes with a start. What the relic showed her of its power: its tale sits like a weight in her gut as she comes around, wondering abstractedly how it ends.

Is its tale a warning or encouragement to proceed cautiously?

She almost laughs, imagining Wolf's reaction when she tells him.

Relic balanced between one finger and thumb, her other hand quests the lobe of her ear in wonder. The smallest things have been known to make a difference. An edge can win a war, even when all is thought to be lost and over.

Maybe the world is not at its end. Maybe all they need is a dragon.

Author Bio

With a keen love of the fantasy genre, Jodie has been writing stories for her own enjoyment since she was eleven.

When she's not writing queer fantasy adventures or reading through a never-ending pile of books, she can generally be found cross-stitching, exploring gardens, immersing herself in video game worlds, or 'conversing' with her favourite chickens. What has she learnt? Always make time for writing.